THE INTERNATIONAL BURRITO

The First Complete Burrito Cookbook—
Over 70 Innovative Recipes

Hillary Davis

WARNER BOOKS

A Time Warner Company

ⓖ ⓙ ⓖ

To my parents, Laura and Hal Davis

Warner Books, Inc., 1271 Avenue of the Americas, New York, NY 10020

Ⓦ A Time Warner Company

Printed in the United States of America
First Printing: November 1994
10 9 8 7 6 5 4 3 2 1

Library of Congress Cataloging-in-Publication Data

Davis, Hillary.
    The international burrito / Hillary Davis.
        p.   cm.
    Includes index.
    ISBN 0-446-67051-0
    1. Burritos (Cookery)   2. Cookery, International.   I. Title.
TX836.D38   1994
641.82—dc20   94-6291
                                                         CIP

Cover design by Julia Kushnirsky

Cover illustration by David Montiel

Book design by Giorgetta Bell McRee

DRESSING UP THE COMMON BURRITO...FOR A CULINARY TRIP

As the burrito has increased in popularity, it has entered the realm of haute cuisine where gourmet chefs have delighted in its infinite adaptability. Now, THE INTERNATIONAL BURRITO shows you how to discover innovative methods for turning the standard Mexican burrito into a culinary adventure of global proportions. Learn how to make tasty, easy, and imaginative dishes, such as:

- **GRILLED CHICKEN-PESTO BURRITO**—Pungent garlic, fresh basil, pine nuts, and Parmesan cheese add a distinctly Italian flavor to chicken marinated in balsamic vinegar and olive oil, then grilled al fresco and sprinkled with fresh chopped tomato. *Salut!*

- **VEGETABLE COUSCOUS BURRITO**—Moroccan couscous is cooked with celery, carrots, turnips, potatoes, and peppers in a rich chicken broth spiced with cayenne and coriander. A nourishing burrito of Middle Eastern persuasion!

- **EGG ROLL BURRITO**—Bean sprouts, soy sauce, and zingy ginger bring the burrito to the Orient in a dish made of pork loin and fresh spinach. Great with hot mustard!

- **CURRIED LAMB BURRITO WITH MANGO CHUTNEY**—Lamb stew curried to perfection and cooked in a chicken-broth–coconut-milk–tomato-paste concoction pays homage to the fine cuisine of India. The result? An exotic burrito topped with toasted coconut, chopped cilantro, and incredible mango chutney!

Acknowledgments

I would like to thank Ling Lucas and Karen Kelly
for helping this book come to be.

Contents

3. Mexico

4. Morocco

5. France

6. Greece

7. China

Before You Begin

How to Warm Tortillas

- **In the Oven**—Preheat the oven to 250° F. Wrap the tortillas in aluminum foil and seal completely. Place in the oven and warm for 10 minutes or until all the tortillas are heated through.

- **In the Microwave**—Wrap the tortillas in several sheets of paper towels and microwave on HIGH for ½ to 1 minute or until warm.

How to Fold a Tortilla into a Burrito

Place an 8- or 10-inch tortilla on a flat surface. Spoon the desired filling in the center of the tortilla, mounding lengthwise. Be careful not to overstuff the tortilla or it might rip open when rolled.

Then fold the right and left sides of the tortilla in toward the center so they just touch the edges of the filling. Holding the sides in place with your fingers, roll up the bottom edge of the tortilla over the filling and toward the top, as if rolling up a cigarette. Place the burrito seam side down in a pan or dish before heating, if necessary, or before serving.

1

India

India is a country whose cuisine is defined by full-bodied spices, among them cumin, coriander, cardamom, turmeric, and cayenne pepper, which when combined make curry powder. These seasonings add an unusual dimension to standard meat and vegetable dishes, which come alive when served in flour tortillas as burritos.

Indian-Style Baked Cabbage Burrito

2 tablespoons butter
5 cups chopped green cabbage

1 large onion, minced
½ cup shredded coconut
1 teaspoon turmeric
¼ teaspoon cayenne pepper
⅛ teaspoon ground cinnamon
1 teaspoon salt
1 cup cold water
12 flour tortillas, warmed

1. Preheat the oven to 450° F.

2. In an ovenproof casserole, combine all the ingredients except the tortillas, and toss to coat. Cover with foil and bake about 30 minutes or until cabbage is fork-tender. Spoon into warmed flour tortillas. Fold burrito style and serve.

Makes 6 servings

Chicken Tandoori Burrito

Marinade

1 teaspoon ground cumin
1 teaspoon ground cardamom
1 teaspoon ground coriander
½ teaspoon ground cinnamon
1 teaspoon ground ginger
2 whole dried chili peppers
1 teaspoon turmeric
½ teaspoon fennel seeds
1 teaspoon ground white pepper
2 tablespoons sweet paprika
1 green bell pepper, cored, seeded, and cut in pieces
1 small onion, quartered
1 cup plain yogurt
1 teaspoon orange food coloring (optional)
1 teaspoon salt

1½ pounds skinless, boneless chicken breast, cut in ½-inch strips
2 tablespoons fresh lemon juice

Raita

1 cup plain yogurt
1 large cucumber, peeled, seeded, and chopped
12 cherry tomatoes, sliced
1 large garlic clove, crushed
2 tablespoons fresh lemon juice
Salt and freshly ground black pepper to taste

16 flour tortillas, warmed

1. Several hours ahead or the night before, combine the first 12 ingredients in the bowl of a food processor fitted with a metal blade or a blender. Blend well. Add the yogurt, food coloring, and salt. Place the chicken in a glass or ceramic bowl and pour lemon juice over top. Toss to coat. Pour the yogurt mixture over the top. Toss well. Cover with plastic wrap and allow to marinate at least 6 hours.

2. To make the raita, combine the yogurt with the cucumber, tomatoes, garlic, and lemon juice. Blend well. Season with salt and pepper.

3. Preheat the broiler. Drain the chicken. Place on a broiler pan lined with aluminum foil and cook 3 to 5 minutes or until chicken is cooked through. Spoon chicken into warmed tortillas. Top with raita, fold as for burritos, then serve.

Makes 8 servings

Kashmiri Kebob Burrito with Ginger

Marinade

3 tablespoons minced fresh ginger
2 large garlic cloves, minced
1 tablespoon hot Madras curry powder
1 teaspoon ground cinnamon
2 teaspoons turmeric
¼ cup fresh lemon juice
1 cup olive oil
2 tablespoons honey
1 teaspoon salt

1½ pounds boneless leg of lamb, cut in ½-inch chunks

Dressing

1 teaspoon turmeric
⅛ teaspoon ground cardamom
½ teaspoon curry powder
1 cup plain yogurt
¼ teaspoon salt
2 tablespoons fresh lemon juice
1 small garlic clove, minced
2 green onions, minced

1 cup cooked Basmati rice
16 whole-wheat tortillas, grilled or warmed in oven

1. Several hours ahead or the night before, combine the ginger, garlic, curry, cinnamon, turmeric, lemon juice, oil, honey, and salt in a large ceramic or glass mixing bowl. Blend well and add the lamb. Marinate for at least 6 hours or overnight.

2. Preheat the broiler or grill. Drain the lamb completely and thread onto metal or wooden skewers. (If using wooden skewers, soak in warm water for at least 30 minutes.) Broil 4 inches from heat source for 5 to 7 minutes, turning occasionally or until meat reaches desired doneness.

3. To make the dressing, combine the turmeric, cardamom, and curry powder in a small, dry skillet over medium heat and toast the spices, stirring constantly with a wooden spoon, about 1 minute or until they are fragrant. Combine the remaining dressing ingredients in a small bowl and stir in the toasted spices.

4. Place the lamb and Basmati rice in warmed tortillas, and spoon dressing on top. Fold as for burritos and serve.

Makes 8 servings

Curried Lamb Burrito with Mango Chutney

3 tablespoons vegetable oil
2 pounds lean boneless leg of lamb, cut in ½-inch cubes
1 large onion, cut in ½-inch cubes
2 large garlic cloves, finely minced
5 medium carrots, peeled, trimmed, and cut in ¼-inch thick slices
2 small red-skinned potatoes, cut in ¼-inch chunks
2 tablespoons hot or mild curry powder, preferably homemade (recipe follows)
1½ cups chicken broth
½ cup sweetened coconut milk
2 teaspoons tomato paste (optional)
1 teaspoon salt
16 to 18 flour tortillas, warmed
¼ cup flaked coconut, toasted
¼ cup chopped cilantro (fresh coriander)
Mango Chutney (recipe follows)

1. Place the oil in a large saucepan over high heat. When oil is hot, cook the lamb in a single layer until nicely browned on all sides. Cook in several batches, if necessary, until all the lamb is browned. Remove seared lamb to platter and set aside.

2. Add the onion to the same pan and cook, stirring, 1 to 2 minutes or until onion is transparent. Add garlic and continue to cook 30 seconds longer.

3. Add carrots and potatoes and stir to coat with oil. Sprinkle vegetables with curry powder and stir to coat. Cook 1 to 2 minutes. This will remove the starchy taste from the curry powder.

4. Stir in chicken broth, coconut milk, tomato paste, and salt. Reduce heat to low and simmer 20 minutes or until slightly thickened. Add lamb and simmer 30 minutes longer or until meat is very tender. Spoon into warmed tortillas with coconut, cilantro, and Mango Chutney. Fold up burrito style and serve.

Makes 8 or 9 servings

⊙ ⊙ ⊙

Curry Powder

1 tablespoon ground coriander
2 tablespoons ground cumin
2 teaspoons fennel seeds
1 tablespoon turmeric
½ teaspoon cayenne pepper
2 cardamom pods
1 tablespoon ground ginger
1 teaspoon ground cinnamon

Combine all the ingredients in a small coffee grinder or in a mortar with pestle, and grind until well blended. Store in an airtight container in a cool place.

Makes about ⅓ cup

Mango Chutney

2 tablespoons vegetable oil
1 medium onion, coarsely chopped
1 large garlic clove, minced
⅛ teaspoon cayenne pepper
2 whole cloves
1 cinnamon stick
1 cardamom pod (optional)
½ cup packed dark brown sugar
¼ cup cider vinegar
1 cup chicken broth
⅓ cup dark raisins
2 fresh mangoes, peeled, pitted, and cut in 1-inch chunks (see Note page 10)

1. Place oil in a medium saucepan over medium heat. When hot, add the onion. Cook, stirring, 1 to 2 minutes or until transparent. Add the garlic and cayenne and cook 1 minute longer.

2. Add the cloves, cinnamon, cardamom, brown sugar, vinegar, broth, and raisins. Bring to a boil. Reduce heat to low and simmer 20 minutes.

3. Add the mangoes and cook 15 minutes longer or until mangoes are soft. Remove from heat and cool to room temperature. Refrigerate overnight to allow flavors to fully develop. Remove cinnamon stick and cardamom pod before serving and bring chutney back to room temperature before serving.

Makes about 2 cups

Note: Mangoes are an unusual fruit in that they have a flat pit that is somewhat difficult to remove from the sweet edible flesh. To do so with the least effort, score the skin with the tip of a sharp knife, starting from the stem end and going completely around the entire fruit, ending at the starting point. Make another cut in the skin so the second cut crosses over and through the first. Peel the skin away from the flesh slowly so you only remove the skin.

Remembering that the pit is flat, cut the fruit away from it making certain that you remove the fruit from the flat side. You can do so in one piece and then cut the flesh into chunks, or you can score the flesh as you did the skin, removing it in quarters and then cutting these in chunks.

East Indian Rice with Lentils Burrito

2 tablespoons butter
1 tablespoon vegetable oil
1 small onion, minced
1 cup dried brown lentils (see Note)
1 cup Basmati rice, rinsed
¼ teaspoon salt
1 teaspoon crushed hot red pepper flakes
1 teaspoon cumin seeds, toasted
1 teaspoon ground coriander
5½ cups chicken or vegetable broth
⅓ cup dark raisins
12 flour tortillas, warmed

1. Place the butter and oil in a medium saucepan over high heat. When hot, add the onion and cook 1 to 2 minutes or until transparent. Stir in the lentils, rice, salt, pepper flakes, cumin seeds, and coriander. Stir to coat with the fat.

2. Add the broth to the rice mixture and bring to a boil. Cover and reduce heat to low. Simmer 20 to 25 minutes, or until all the liquid is absorbed and the rice and lentils are cooked. Stir in raisins. Spoon into warmed tortillas, fold up burrito style, and serve.

Makes 6 servings

Note: Lentils come in a variety of sizes and colors, including green, yellow, orange, and brown. The yellow, orange, and green lentils have a milder flavor than the brown ones and are more fragile when cooked. They tend to fall apart and get mushy, unlike the brown ones recommended for this recipe.

Sweet Spiced Yogurt-Cheese Burrito

4 cups plain yogurt
6 tablespoons granulated sugar
1 teaspoon ground cardamom
¼ teaspoon freshly grated nutmeg
½ teaspoon ground cinnamon
½ teaspoon saffron threads, soaked in 1 tablespoon warm water, or 1 teaspoon turmeric (see Note)
¼ cup chopped pistachios
6 fresh figs, sliced, or 8 dried figs, chopped
2 tablespoons confectioners' sugar
8 flour tortillas, warmed

1. Several hours ahead, or the night before, wrap the yogurt in cheesecloth, or place it in a paper coffee filter in a bowl, and allow the liquid (whey) to drain from it.

2. Transfer the drained yogurt to a small bowl. Stir in the sugar, cardamom, nutmeg, cinnamon, saffron, and pistachios. Blend well. Spread on tortilla and layer figs on top of yogurt. Roll up tortilla and sprinkle on top with confectioners' sugar.

Makes 8 servings

Note: Turmeric is sometimes referred to as Indian saffron, and can be used in place of the more rare and expensive spice. It is easily recognized by its bright yellow color.

2

Italy

While Catherine de Medici would not have known what a tortilla was, she could not have disputed its use as a wrapper for such classic Italian dishes as osso buco or shrimp fra diavolo—even cannoli can be a type of burrito.

Antipasto Burrito

Salad

1 6-ounce jar marinated artichoke hearts, drained and quartered
12 cherry tomatoes, sliced
1 green bell pepper, cored, seeded, and chopped
1 pound fresh mozzarella, cut in ¼-inch cubes
1 cup marinated mushrooms, halved
1 cup oil-cured olives, pitted and chopped
½ cup pepperoncini peppers, destemmed and quartered
½ pound Genoa salami, in one piece, cut in ¼-inch cubes
12 flour tortillas, warmed

Dressing

2 tablespoons red wine vinegar
1 large garlic clove, minced
1 teaspoon chopped fresh oregano (see Note), or ¼ teaspoon dried
¼ cup extra-virgin olive oil
Salt and freshly ground black pepper to taste

1. Combine the salad ingredients in a large bowl and toss together.

2. In a small bowl, whisk together the dressing ingredients. Add to the salad and toss to coat. Spoon immediately into warmed tortillas, fold up burrito style, and serve.

Makes 6 servings

Note: Although tastes vary, generally use one-third the amount of fresh when substituting with dried herbs. For example, if a recipe calls for 1 tablespoon fresh herbs, you could substitute 1 teaspoon dried. Of course, this is only a guideline; when I use fresh herbs, I use a lot, so this formula does not always work for me.

Grilled Chicken-Pesto Burrito

Marinade

¼ cup balsamic vinegar
½ cup extra-virgin olive oil
1 teaspoon salt
¼ teaspoon freshly ground black pepper
1 pound skinless, boneless chicken breast

Pesto

3 large garlic cloves
3 cups firmly packed fresh basil leaves, plus 6 extra whole basil leaves for
    optional garnish
¼ cup pine nuts, toasted (see Note)
½ cup grated Parmesan cheese
1 cup extra-virgin olive oil
Salt and freshly ground pepper to taste

12 flour tortillas, warmed
1 large tomato, coarsely chopped

1. To marinate chicken, combine the vinegar, olive oil, salt, and pepper in a medium glass or ceramic bowl. Add the chicken, toss to coat, and cover bowl with plastic wrap. Marinate 2 hours at room temperature.

2. Meanwhile, in the bowl of a food processor or blender, make the pesto by combining the garlic, basil, pine nuts, and Parmesan cheese. Blend the basil-cheese mixture until well chopped. With processor still running, slowly add the olive oil in a thin stream until a smooth paste forms. Transfer pesto to a medium mixing bowl. Season with salt and pepper.

3. Preheat the broiler or prepare an outdoor grill. Remove chicken from marinade and pat dry with paper towels. When grill or broiler is hot, cook chicken 3 to 5 minutes on each side or until just cooked through. Do not overcook. Remove from heat and let cool 2 to 3 minutes before slicing.

4. Cut chicken into thin strips. Add chicken to the pesto. Spoon chicken pesto into tortillas and sprinkle with chopped tomato. Garnish with extra basil leaves, if desired. Roll up burrito style and serve.

Makes 6 servings

Note: To toast nuts, preheat the oven to 350° F. Place nuts on a small pie plate or jelly-roll pan, depending on how many nuts you need to toast. Place in oven and cook 7 to 10 minutes or until the nuts begin to turn golden. Shake the pan occasionally during cooking time so they brown evenly. When the nuts are starting to brown, remove from oven, since the heat of the pan will continue to cook them.

Osso Buco Burrito

Osso Buco

½ cup all-purpose flour
1 teaspoon salt
¼ teaspoon freshly ground black pepper
1½ pounds boneless veal shank meat, cut in ½-inch pieces
3 tablespoons vegetable oil
1 10-ounce package frozen pearl onions, thawed
2 large carrots, peeled, trimmed, and cut into ½-inch chunks
1 large celery stalk, cut in ½-inch chunks
¾ teaspoon ground sage
½ teaspoon dried thyme
1 teaspoon crushed dried rosemary
3 large garlic cloves, crushed
1 cup chicken broth
½ cup dry white wine
1 tablespoon tomato paste
Salt and pepper to taste

Gremolata Topping

⅓ cup grated lemon rind
½ cup chopped fresh parsley
2 large garlic cloves, finely minced
Salt and freshly ground black pepper to taste

16 to 18 flour tortillas, warmed

ⓖ ⓙ ⓖ

1. Season flour with salt and pepper. Dredge meat on all sides, shaking off any excess flour. Pour oil into a large casserole with a lid. Place over high heat; when oil is hot, add meat in one layer, cooking in several batches, if necessary. Cook 3 to 5 minutes or until meat is golden brown on all sides. Carefully remove cooked meat to a plate. Set aside.

2. Reduce heat to medium. To the same pan add the onions, carrots, and celery. Cover casserole and cook 10 minutes, stirring occasionally. Stir in sage, thyme, rosemary, and garlic. Cook 2 to 3 minutes or until herbs become fragrant. Add broth, wine, and tomato paste. Bring to a boil. Reduce heat to low and simmer 5 minutes.

3. Add reserved meat with any juices to the pot. Cover and simmer 45 minutes or until meat is very tender.

4. Meanwhile, make the gremolata. In a small bowl, combine the lemon rind, parsley, garlic, salt, and pepper. Set aside.

5. Remove stew from heat. Adjust seasonings with salt and freshly ground black pepper.

6. Spoon osso buco filling into the center of each warmed tortilla and sprinkle with some of the gremolata. Roll up as for burrito and serve immediately.

Makes 8 or 9 servings

Quick Pizza Burrito

Sauce

2 tablespoons olive oil
4 large garlic cloves, crushed
¼ cup sun-dried tomatoes in oil (see Note), chopped
2 cups tomato puree
1 teaspoon dried basil
½ teaspoon dried oregano
½ teaspoon dried thyme
1 tablespoon tomato paste
1 teaspoon sugar
½ teaspoon freshly ground black pepper

16 flour tortillas

Toppings

Grated Parmesan and mozzarella cheese
Goat cheese
Sautéed onions, peppers, wild and domestic mushrooms, spinach
Steamed broccoli
Pepperoni

1. Pour the oil into a medium saucepan placed over medium heat. When hot, add the garlic and cook, stirring constantly, for 30 seconds. Add the tomatoes and cook 3 minutes longer. Stir in the tomato puree, basil, oregano, and thyme. Cover, reduce heat to low, and cook 15 to 20 minutes. Stir in tomato paste and sugar, and simmer 5 minutes longer. Remove from heat.

2. Preheat the oven to 375° F.

3. Place 2 tablespoons sauce on each flour tortilla. Add the desired fillings, roll up burrito style, place on a cookie sheet, and heat 5 to 10 minutes or until fillings are thoroughly warmed.

Makes 8 servings

Note: Make your own sun-dried tomatoes in oil. You can often find loose sun-dried tomatoes in bags. Reconstitute them by placing them in a glass container fitted with a lid and cover with olive oil. You can also use the olive oil to flavor salads and pastas.

Italian Sausage and Peppers Burrito

1 tablespoon olive oil
1½ pounds hot Italian sausage
2 large onions, thinly sliced
1 large garlic clove, minced
1 tablespoon chopped fresh oregano, or 1 teaspoon dried
1 large red bell pepper, cored, seeded, and chopped
1 large green bell pepper, cored, seeded, and chopped
1 large yellow bell pepper, cored, seeded, and chopped
1 teaspoon fennel seeds
Salt and freshly ground black pepper to taste
16 flour tortillas, warmed

1. Place oil in a large skillet over high heat. When hot, add the sausage and cook about 10 to 15 minutes or until golden brown on all sides and cooked through. Transfer cooked sausage to a plate.

2. Add onions to the same pan. Cook about 10 minutes, stirring occasionally, or until brown. Add the garlic and cook 1 minute longer. Add the oregano, peppers, and fennel seeds. Reduce the heat to medium and cook about 5 minutes or until peppers are just tender.

3. While the peppers are cooking, cut the cooked sausage in bite-size pieces. Return these to the pan and cook until heated through. Season with salt and pepper. Spoon into warmed tortillas, fold up burrito style, and serve immediately.

Makes 8 servings

Rollatini di Pollo Burrito

Chicken

4 8-ounce skinless, boneless chicken breasts
1 tablespoon olive oil
1 small onion, minced
2 large garlic cloves, minced
1 tablespoon chopped fresh oregano, or 1 teaspoon dried
1 10-ounce package frozen chopped spinach or chopped broccoli, thawed and squeezed dry
1 cup whole-milk ricotta cheese
2 eggs, lightly beaten
½ cup seasoned dry bread crumbs
¼ teaspoon salt
½ teaspoon ground black pepper
¼ cup grated Parmesan cheese

Sauce

2 cups tomato puree
1 tablespoon sugar
2 tablespoons balsamic vinegar
1 tablespoon tomato paste
¼ teaspoon freshly ground black pepper
2 large tomatoes, chopped
¼ cup chopped fresh basil or parsley

12 flour tortillas, warmed
Fresh spinach leaves (optional)

1. Preheat the oven to 350° F.

2. Place the chicken breasts between 2 pieces of waxed paper and pound slightly to flatten with a meat mallet.

3. Add oil to a small sauté pan set over high heat. When hot, add the onion and cook 1 to 2 minutes, stirring constantly, or until transparent. Add the garlic and cook for 1 minute longer. Remove from heat. Let cool slightly, then add the oregano, spinach or broccoli, ricotta, eggs, bread crumbs, salt, pepper, and Parmesan. Blend well.

4. Divide mixture evenly among the chicken breasts, making certain to mound spinach mixture lengthwise. Roll breasts up over filling and place on a baking sheet lined with aluminum foil. Bake for 25 to 30 minutes or until cooked through.

5. Make the sauce. In a small saucepan, place the tomato puree, sugar, vinegar, tomato paste, and pepper over high heat. Bring to a boil, then reduce heat to low and simmer 15 to 20 minutes. Remove from heat and add fresh tomato and basil or parsley.

6. Thinly slice the rolled chicken breast and place about 3 to 4 slices in the center of each tortilla. Spoon some tomato sauce over the top and layer fresh spinach leaves over the sauce. Fold up burrito style and serve immediately.

Makes 6 servings

Shrimp Fra Diavolo Burrito

3 tablespoons extra-virgin olive oil
1½ pounds medium shrimp, peeled and deveined (see Note page 46), and cut in
   small pieces
1 medium onion, finely minced
3 large garlic cloves, minced
2 hot dried chili peppers, crushed
1 14½-ounce can whole tomatoes in juice
½ cup dry white wine
2 tablespoons fresh lemon juice
¼ teaspoon freshly ground black pepper
1 tablespoon capers, chopped
2 large tomatoes, chopped
½ cup chopped fresh basil or parsley
2 tablespoons balsamic vinegar
¼ teaspoon salt
16 flour tortillas, warmed

1. Place 1 tablespoon of the oil in a large skillet over high heat. When hot, add the shrimp and cook about 5 minutes, stirring constantly, or until slightly pink in color. Remove shrimp from pan with a slotted spoon and transfer to a plate.

2. Add the remaining 2 tablespoons oil and cook the onion 3 to 5 minutes or until transparent. Add the garlic and peppers and continue cooking 3 to 5 minutes longer. Stir in the canned tomatoes, wine, lemon juice, pepper, capers, and tomatoes. Simmer 20 minutes or until slightly thickened. Remove from heat. Stir in the basil or parsley, vinegar, salt, and shrimp. Stir until the shrimp are heated through. Spoon into warmed tortillas, fold burrito style, and serve.

Makes 8 servings

⑤ ⑨ ⑥

Toasted Almond Cannoli

Almond Cream

⅓ cup granulated sugar
4 tablespoons cornstarch
8 egg yolks
2 cups light cream
¼ cup almond-flavored liqueur, or 1 teaspoon almond extract

Tortilla Cannoli

6 flour tortillas
6 wooden toothpicks
½ cup sliced almonds, toasted and crushed
Confectioners' sugar

1. Make the pastry cream by combining the granulated sugar, cornstarch, and yolks in a mixing bowl. In a saucepan, scald the cream over medium-high heat. Do not boil.

2. Slowly add the scalded cream to the egg mixture, blending quickly with a wire whisk. Return this egg-cream mixture to the saucepan over medium-high heat and cook, stirring constantly, until thickened. (Be careful not to boil or you will scramble the eggs.) Remove from the heat and stir in the liqueur or extract. Place a sheet of plastic wrap directly on the surface to prevent a skin from forming and refrigerate while making the tortilla cannoli.

3. Preheat the oven to 350° F.

4. Roll the tortillas into cylinders approximately 2½ inches in diameter and hold them in this shape by securing with a toothpick. Place them on a cookie sheet and bake 5 to 7 minutes or until lightly golden and crisp. When cooked, remove from oven and cool completely. Remove toothpicks.

5. Fill a pastry bag fitted with a plain tip with the pastry cream. Pipe the chilled cream into center of each rolled tortilla. Dip each open end in the almonds, and sprinkle the cannoli with confectioners' sugar.

Makes 6 servings

Note: To save time, substitute the almond cream with 2 packages of instant vanilla pudding, regular or low-calorie. Add 1 teaspoon almond extract or almond-flavored liqueur.

3

Mexico

Mexico is a land steeped in tradition and ritual. It is also a nation quite colorful in its art, architecture, and food. The national bread—the tortilla—acts as a canvas for the creative home chef to make adventurous meals such as you are likely to find in the following pages.

Guacamole Burrito

4 large, ripe Haas avocados, peeled and pitted (see Note)
1 large red onion, finely minced
2 large garlic cloves, minced
¼ cup fresh lemon juice
1 teaspoon salt
½ teaspoon hot red pepper sauce
½ cup chopped cilantro leaves
1 large tomato, chopped
16 flour tortillas, warmed
¼ cup sour cream
1 cup finely shredded romaine lettuce

1. Cut the avocados into large chunks and place them in a large mixing bowl. Smash with a wooden spoon until all the large pieces are gone but avocados are still chunky.

2. Add the onion, garlic, lemon juice, salt, pepper sauce, cilantro, and tomato. Blend well. Place plastic wrap directly on surface and let sit at room temperature for 1 hour to develop flavors.

3. Spoon the guacamole into the centers of the warmed tortillas. Top with sour cream and shredded lettuce. Fold up burrito style and serve immediately.

Makes 8 servings

Note: Haas avocados are recognizable by their black and bumpy outer skin. They have a full, buttery flavor.

Keep guacamole from browning too quickly by adding the avocado pits to the bowl of finished avocado mix. You can also squeeze a little extra lemon juice over the top of the guacamole and then cover surface with plastic wrap.

Grilled Shrimp Burrito

Marinade

¼ cup fresh lime juice (see Note page 32)
1 tablespoon ground coriander
1 teaspoon dried epazote (see Note opposite) (optional)
1 chipotle pepper
1 cup safflower oil
1 teaspoon salt

16 jumbo shrimp, peeled and deveined (see Note page 46), and halved
    horizontally

Salsa

4 large tomatoes, chopped
1 small red onion, minced
1 large garlic clove, minced
2 green onions, minced
2 tablespoons balsamic vinegar
1 teaspoon hot red pepper sauce
¼ teaspoon salt

16 flour tortillas, warmed
½ cup cilantro leaves

1. In a small saucepan, combine the lime juice, coriander, epazote, chipotle pepper, oil, and salt. Bring to a boil over high heat and cook 1 to 2 minutes. Remove from heat and cool to room temperature. Place the shrimp in a glass or ceramic dish and pour the marinade over top. Toss and refrigerate for 1 hour. (Make certain you don't over-marinate. Maximum marination time should not exceed 1 hour, since the acid tends to cook the shrimp, and if left to marinate too long will make it fall apart and have a mushy texture.)

2. Drain shrimp. Preheat the broiler or prepare a charcoal grill. When hot, cook shrimp 4 inches from the heat source for about 3 minutes or until just opaque. Be careful not to overcook.

3. While shrimp are cooking, combine salsa ingredients in a small bowl and mix well.

4. Spoon shrimp into warmed tortillas topped with cilantro leaves and salsa. Fold as for a burrito and serve.

Makes 8 servings

Note: Epazote is a spice unique to Mexican cuisine, which is available in Spanish groceries.

Red Snapper Burrito with Red Hot Sauce

½ cup olive oil
1 large onion, finely minced
2 tablespoons chopped cilantro, plus ¼ cup cilantro leaves for optional garnish
¼ teaspoon cayenne pepper
1 red bell pepper, cored, seeded, and chopped
1 green bell pepper, cored, seeded, and chopped
2 medium tomatoes, chopped
1 cup fresh lime juice (see Note)
2 whole red snappers, about 2 pounds each, filleted
16 flour tortillas, warmed

1. Preheat the oven to 375° F.

2. Place the oil in a medium saucepan over high heat. When hot, add the onion and cook, stirring, 3 to 5 minutes or until transparent. Stir in 2 tablespoons cilantro, cayenne, and peppers. Cook 5 minutes, stirring occasionally. Stir in the tomatoes and lime juice and bring the sauce to a boil. Reduce heat to low and simmer 20 to 25 minutes.

3. Place the fish on a foil-covered baking pan. Pour the sauce over fish and bake for 15 minutes or until fish flakes easily with a fork. Spoon into warmed tortillas and sprinkle with cilantro leaves, if desired. Fold into burritos and serve.

Makes 8 servings

Note: When extracting juice from fresh limes, preheat the oven to low and place limes on an ovenproof dish. Heat for several minutes, then remove from oven. Using the palm of your hand, roll the limes on a hard surface to loosen the pulp. Cut the limes in half, then squeeze juice by hand, juicer, or reamer. If the limes are juicy, you should be able to get about 2 to 3 tablespoons juice from each lime.

Spicy Mexican Eggs Burrito

2 tablespoons butter
¼ cup minced onion
1 large garlic clove, minced
½ fresh jalapeño pepper, minced (see Note)
¼ cup chopped pimiento
6 ounces diced ham or chorizo sausage
8 eggs, lightly beaten
Salt and pepper to taste
12 flour tortillas, warmed
¼ cup chopped cilantro

1. Melt the butter in a large, nonstick skillet over high heat. Add the onion, garlic, jalapeño, pimiento, and ham. Cook, stirring constantly, 2 to 3 minutes or until onion is transparent.

2. Reduce heat to medium-low. Add eggs and cook, stirring slowly but constantly, until they have a creamy consistency. Season with salt and pepper.

3. Spoon the eggs into the tortillas and sprinkle with cilantro. Fold as for burritos and serve immediately.

Makes 6 servings

Note: Remember, you can never be too careful when handling these hot peppers. Use a pair of rubber gloves when seeding them and make certain you clean all surfaces after handling. If you don't have rubber gloves, wash your hands thoroughly with soap and water. Keep the peppers away from mucous membranes.

Bean and Cheese Burrito
with Toasted Cumin Seeds

2 tablespoons butter
1 jalapeño pepper, seeded and finely minced (see Note page 33)
1 large garlic clove, minced
1 tablespoon cumin seeds, toasted
1 teaspoon dry mustard
2 tablespoons flour
1 cup milk
2 teaspoons Worcestershire sauce
⅛ teaspoon cayenne pepper
¾ cup grated sharp cheddar cheese
½ cup grated Monterey Jack cheese
2 cups cooked black beans
¼ teaspoon salt
16 flour tortillas, warmed
½ cup mint leaves
1 cup tomato salsa (optional)

1. Preheat the oven to 400° F.

2. Place butter in a medium saucepan over high heat. When hot, add the jalapeño and garlic and cook 1 to 2 minutes. Stir in the cumin seeds and mustard and cook 1 minute longer. Stir in flour and cook 2 to 3 minutes, stirring constantly with a wooden spoon.

3. Using a wire whisk, slowly stir in the milk so there are no lumps. Add the Worcestershire sauce and cayenne. Reduce heat to low and cook 15 to 20 minutes or until mixture gets thick and coats the back of a spoon.

4. Remove pan from heat and stir in cheeses until just melted. Add the beans and salt. Spoon the mixture into the centers of the tortillas and roll up burrito style.

5. Place burritos in a baking dish large enough to hold them in a single layer. Bake for 5 minutes or until heated through. Serve with mint leaves and salsa, if desired.

Makes 8 servings

Chile con Queso Burrito

2 tablespoons vegetable oil
1 large onion, sliced
2 large tomatoes, seeded and chopped
2 3½-ounce cans green chilies
Salt and pepper to taste
8 ounces fresh Mexican-style cheese (*queso fresca*), or 1 8-ounce package
   cream cheese, cut in small pieces
½ cup heavy cream
12 flour tortillas, warmed

1. Place oil in a large skillet over medium heat. When hot, add the onion and cook, stirring, 3 to 5 minutes, or until onion is transparent. Stir in tomatoes and chilies; season with salt and pepper. Cook about 15 minutes or until slightly thickened.

2. Add the cheese to the skillet, and when it begins to melt, add the cream until heated through. Use to fill warmed tortillas and roll up burrito style.

Makes 6 servings

Chicken Burrito with Mole Poblano

1 13¾-ounce can chicken broth
3 ounces dried ancho pepper (see Note)
1 medium onion, finely minced
2 small tomatoes, quartered
½ cup seedless raisins
4 garlic cloves
¼ teaspoon ground cinnamon
½ teaspoon ground coriander
4 ounces unsweetened chocolate, grated
½ teaspoon salt
¼ teaspoon freshly ground black pepper
2 pounds skinless, boneless chicken breasts
16 flour tortillas, warmed
Cilantro leaves

1. In a medium saucepan, combine the broth and the chilies and heat over high heat. When hot but not boiling, turn off the heat and allow the chilies to steep for 10 minutes or until soft. Reserve the broth and remove the chilies. Destem and remove all the seeds from the chilies.

2. Combine the onion, tomatoes, raisins, garlic, cinnamon, and ground coriander in the bowl of a food processor or blender and puree until smooth. Add the reserved chilies and the chicken stock and blend well. Transfer the mixture to a medium saucepan and simmer 15 to 20 minutes over medium heat, stirring constantly.

3. Add the chocolate to the saucepan, reduce heat to low, and cover the pan. Cook 1 to 2 minutes, stirring occasionally, until the chocolate is melted. Season with salt and pepper. Keep mole sauce warm while preparing the chicken.

4. Preheat the broiler or prepare a charcoal grill. When hot, cook the chicken on each side 3 to 5 minutes or until juices run clear when pierced with the tines of a fork. Slice the chicken on an angle, place in the warmed tortillas, and spread with mole sauce. Garnish with cilantro leaves, then fold up burrito style and serve.

Makes 8 servings

Note: Ancho peppers are among the most used of dried red chilies. They are usually quite large, broad, full flavored, and mild.

Drunken Chicken Burrito

2 tablespoons vegetable oil
1 tablespoon butter
1½ pounds skinless, boneless chicken breasts, cut in ½-inch pieces
½ cup cubed ham
1 cup dark raisins
¼ teaspoon ground cloves
½ teaspoon ground cinnamon
1 teaspoon ground cumin
½ teaspoon ground coriander
2 large garlic cloves, crushed
1 cup dry white wine
Salt and pepper to taste
½ cup sliced pimiento-stuffed olives
12 to 16 flour tortillas, warmed

1. Place the oil and butter in a heavy-duty casserole fitted with a lid. Place over high heat; when hot, add chicken and cook, stirring, 3 to 5 minutes or until golden brown.

2. Reduce heat to low and stir in the ham, raisins, cloves, cinnamon, cumin, coriander, garlic, and wine. Cover and simmer 20 to 30 minutes or until chicken is tender. Season with salt and pepper and stir in olives. Spoon into tortillas and fold burrito style.

Makes 6 to 8 servings

Creamy Chicken and Hot Chili Burrito

¼ cup vegetable oil
1 pound skinless, boneless chicken, dark and light meat,
   cut in ¼- to ½-inch cubes
2 chipotle peppers
1 medium onion, cut in 1-inch cubes
2 large garlic cloves, minced
1 jalapeño pepper, seeded and finely minced (see Note page 33)
1 large red bell pepper, cored, seeded, and cut in ½-inch chunks
½ cup chicken broth
1 teaspoon grated lime zest
¼ cup fresh lime juice (see Note page 32)
2 cups heavy cream
¼ teaspoon salt
2 tablespoons chopped fresh parsley
12 flour tortillas, warmed

1. Place oil in a medium skillet over high heat. When hot, add chicken and cook 5 to 7 minutes or until golden brown on all sides. Remove with a slotted spoon to a platter and keep warm.

2. Add the chipotle pepper, onion, garlic, jalapeño pepper, and red pepper to the skillet and cook 3 to 5 minutes or until red pepper starts to soften. Stir in chicken broth, lime zest, and lime juice. Bring to a boil, reduce heat to low, and simmer 10 minutes or until reduced by half.

3. Add the cream to the skillet and continue to cook 15 minutes or until cream is reduced and thickened. Add reserved chicken and any juices to skillet. Season with salt and sprinkle with parsley. Spoon immediately into warmed tortillas, then fold burrito style and serve.

Makes 6 servings

4

Morocco

Though Morocco is located in the northwest corner of Africa, its food has been greatly influenced by the French. Ingredients that include nuts, dried fruit, cinnamon, and couscous create dishes unique to this part of the world and are outstanding elements for burritos.

Lamb Meatball Burritos Scented with Cumin

Meatballs

1 pound ground lamb
1 tablespoon ground cumin
¼ teaspoon cayenne pepper
2 large garlic cloves, minced
2 tablespoons olive oil
2 tablespoons chopped fresh thyme, or 2 teaspoons dried
¼ teaspoon ground cinnamon
1 teaspoon salt
⅛ teaspoon ground black pepper

Dressing

1 cup plain yogurt
1 garlic clove, minced
2 teaspoons ground cumin
2 tablespoons fresh lemon juice
½ teaspoon sugar
3 tablespoons chopped fresh mint
Salt and freshly ground black pepper to taste

12 flour tortillas, warmed
1 small head iceberg lettuce, shredded

1. Preheat the oven to 375° F.

2. In a large mixing bowl, combine the lamb with the next 8 ingredients. Mix well, then form into 1-inch balls (see Note) and place on an ungreased baking sheet. Bake for 5 to 10 minutes or until they are desired doneness.

3. Meanwhile, prepare dressing in a small bowl. Combine yogurt, garlic, cumin, lemon juice, sugar, mint, salt, and pepper. Mix well.

4. Place meatballs in warmed tortillas and sprinkle with shredded lettuce and cumin dressing. Fold burrito style and serve.

Makes 6 servings

Note: Making meatballs can be easy if you use a meatballer specifically for this purpose. You can find them at houseware stores and in some supermarkets.

Moroccan Eggplant Burrito

2 large eggplants, cut in ½-inch cubes
½ cup olive oil
1 small onion, minced
1 tablespoon minced fresh ginger
2 large garlic cloves, minced
1 teaspoon turmeric
¼ teaspoon cayenne pepper
¼ teaspoon ground cinnamon
2 large tomatoes, seeded and chopped
¼ teaspoon salt
½ teaspoon freshly ground black pepper
1 tablespoon sesame seeds, toasted
16 whole-wheat tortillas, warmed

1. Place the eggplant cubes in a colander. Salt generously and allow to drain for 30 minutes, then rinse thoroughly under cold water (see Note).

2. Place oil in a large skillet over high heat. When hot, add eggplant and cook, stirring constantly, 7 to 10 minutes or until soft. Add the onion, ginger, garlic, turmeric, cayenne, and cinnamon. Cook 5 minutes longer or until onion has wilted slightly. Reduce heat to medium; add tomatoes, salt, and pepper. Simmer 20 minutes.

3. Remove skillet from heat and sprinkle mixture with sesame seeds. Spoon into warmed tortillas, then fold burrito style and serve.

Makes 8 servings

Note: Sometimes eggplants can be bitter, depending on how old they are. The salt helps extract the bitterness and extra moisture. Rinsing the eggplant before use removes the salt.

Lemon Chicken Burrito with Olives

2 pounds skinless, boneless chicken, dark and light meat, cut in 2-inch strips
3 small lemons, thinly sliced, or salt-preserved lemons (see Note page 44)
4 large garlic cloves, crushed
¼ cup olive oil
1½ teaspoons ground ginger
1 teaspoon turmeric
½ teaspoon coarsely ground black pepper
1 teaspoon salt
1 large onion, thinly sliced
½ cup chopped fresh parsley
¼ cup cilantro leaves
3 tablespoons butter, sliced
1 cup oil-cured olives, pitted and coarsely chopped
16 flour tortillas

1. In a large mixing bowl, combine the chicken with the lemons, half the garlic, and the oil, ginger, turmeric, pepper, and salt. Toss to coat well.

2. Arrange the chicken in a casserole fitted with a lid. Top with the onion, parsley, cilantro, and butter. Add 2 cups water. Cover pot, bring to a boil over high heat, and reduce to a simmer. Simmer 45 minutes to 1 hour or until chicken is tender.

3. Transfer chicken to a serving dish and keep warm while finishing the sauce. Add the olives to the casserole and increase the heat to medium-high. Cook the sauce about 5 minutes or until slightly thickened.

4. Pour sauce over chicken and place in warmed tortillas. Fold burrito style and serve immediately.

Makes 8 servings

Note: Salt-preserved lemons are classically used in this dish. They are easy to make but take a couple of weeks to cure. Place 4 lemons on their stem ends. Make a cut down the center of each lemon to within ¼ inch of the base. Do not cut all the way through. Make a quarter turn and make another cut the same way. Using a glass jar fitted with a lid, and large enough to hold all the lemons, spread a layer of coarse salt in the bottom. Pack each lemon cut with salt and then place in the jar. Then cover with salt. Cover and keep in a cool place for 2 weeks. Rinse thoroughly before using. The lemons are great in baked fish dishes, salads, and marinades.

Vegetable Couscous Burrito

2 tablespoons olive oil
1 medium onion, finely minced
2 medium garlic cloves, minced
¼ teaspoon cayenne pepper
¼ teaspoon ground coriander
1 cardamom pod (optional)
2 celery stalks, cut in ¼-inch cubes
2 large carrots, peeled and cut in ¼-inch cubes
2 medium turnips, peeled and cut in ¼-inch cubes
2 medium potatoes, peeled and cut in ¼-inch cubes
2 red bell peppers, cored, seeded, and cut in ¼-inch cubes
5 cups chicken broth
2 cups quick-cooking couscous
16 to 20 flour tortillas, warmed
2 small tomatoes, chopped
½ cup chopped fresh parsley

1. Place oil in a large saucepan over high heat. When hot, add onion and cook 3 to 5 minutes, stirring constantly, or until onion is transparent. Stir in garlic, cayenne, coriander, and cardamom pod, if using. Cook 30 seconds.

2. Add the celery, carrots, turnips, potatoes, and peppers. Cook, stirring constantly, for 5 minutes or until vegetables begin to brown. Stir in chicken broth and bring to boil over high heat. Reduce heat to low and cover. Simmer 7 to 10 minutes or until vegetables are tender.

3. Remove lid and stir in couscous. Cover and remove from heat. Let sit 3 to 5 minutes or until the liquid is absorbed and couscous is plumped and tender.

4. Spoon vegetable couscous into the centers of warmed tortillas and top with chopped tomatoes and parsley. Roll up burrito style and serve.

Makes 8 to 10 servings

Shrimp Tajine Burrito

¼ teaspoon ground black pepper
½ teaspoon salt
2 tablespoons ground cumin
1 teaspoon ground ginger
½ teaspoon turmeric
1 teaspoon ground cinnamon
1½ pounds medium shrimp, peeled and deveined (see Note)
¼ cup olive oil
1 large onion, finely minced
4 large tomatoes, chopped
1 tablespoon tomato paste
½ pound green beans, trimmed and cut in ½-inch lengths
¼ cup chopped fresh parsley
1 tablespoon sesame seeds, toasted (optional)
16 flour tortillas, warmed

1. In a large mixing bowl, combine the pepper, salt, cumin, ginger, turmeric, and cinnamon. Add the shrimp and toss to coat, shaking off any excess. In a large skillet, heat the oil over high heat. When hot, add the shrimp and sauté 2 to 3 minutes, stirring constantly, or until shrimp starts to turn pink.

2. Add the onion and continue to cook, stirring constantly, 3 to 5 minutes. Reduce heat to medium and add tomatoes, tomato paste, and beans. Cook 5 minutes longer or until the beans are fork-tender. Sprinkle with parsley and toasted sesame seeds, if desired. Spoon into warmed tortillas. Fold up burrito style and serve immediately.

Makes 8 servings

Note: To peel and devein shrimp, remove the shell from shrimp by first taking off the legs. Starting from the head, carefully peel the shell from the body. Spread the tail section and gently pull the shell from side to side to loosen, then remove. When deveining, you need remove only the vein from the top of the shrimp. Using a sharp paring knife, make a small incision along the entire length of the top of the shrimp and remove the small black vein. Discard.

5

France

Thought by many to have some of the best cuisine in the world, France has a number of dishes that make excellent burrito fillings. Of course, don't tell a Frenchman this.

Alsatian Onion and Potato Burrito

4 tablespoons (½ stick) butter
2 large onions, thinly sliced
2 garlic cloves, minced
4 large all-purpose potatoes, peeled and cut in ¼-inch cubes
½ teaspoon dried thyme
1 teaspoon anise seeds
1 teaspoon salt
½ cup Gewürztraminer wine
1 cup heavy cream
1 cup grated Gruyère cheese
¼ cup grated Parmesan cheese
2 tablespoons chopped fresh parsley
16 to 18 flour tortillas, warmed

1. Preheat the broiler.

2. Place the butter in a large ovenproof skillet over high heat. When it has melted and begins to brown, add the onions and cook 5 to 7 minutes or until soft. Add the garlic and cook, stirring constantly, for 1 minute. Add the potatoes, thyme, anise seeds, and salt. Stir to coat. Add wine and bring to a boil. Reduce heat to medium, cover, and simmer 10 minutes or until potatoes are tender.

3. Add the cream to the skillet and continue cooking until liquid reduces and coats the back of a spoon. Remove pan from heat, stir in cheeses, and place under broiler until surface is golden brown. Remove from broiler.

4. Sprinkle mixture with parsley and allow to sit at room temperature for several minutes before spooning into warmed tortillas. Fold burrito style and serve.

Makes 8 to 10 servings

Boeuf Bourguignon Burrito

3 tablespoons butter
2 tablespoons vegetable oil
1½ pounds lean stewing beef, cut in ¼- to ½-inch cubes
2 large garlic cloves, crushed
1 teaspoon dried thyme
½ teaspoon dried basil
½ cup all-purpose flour
3 cups red Burgundy wine
2 tablespoons tomato paste
2 cups sliced fresh mushrooms
1 cup frozen pearl onions, thawed
2 large carrots, peeled and cut in ½-inch cubes
½ cup diced slab bacon, in ¼-inch pieces
1 teaspoon salt
¼ teaspoon freshly ground black pepper
2 cups steamed white rice or cooked egg noodles (optional)
½ cup chopped fresh parsley
16 to 20 flour tortillas, warmed

1. Place butter and oil in a large saucepan over high heat. When hot, add the beef and cook 5 to 7 minutes or until nicely browned. Add garlic and cook, stirring, 30 seconds longer. Add thyme and basil and cook 2 to 3 minutes, stirring constantly. Add flour and cook 3 minutes longer, stirring constantly.

2. Stir in the red wine and tomato paste. Bring to a boil; reduce heat to low and simmer 5 minutes. Add the mushrooms, onions, carrots, and bacon. Cover pan and cook about 30 minutes or until beef and vegetables are tender, stirring occasionally. Season with salt and pepper.

3. Place the beef mixture over the rice or noodles, if desired, in warmed tortillas. Sprinkle with chopped parsley and fold burrito style. Serve immediately.

Makes 8 to 10 servings

Chicken Chasseur Burrito

1 pound skinless, boneless chicken, dark and white meat, cut in ½-inch cubes
½ teaspoon salt
¼ teaspoon coarsely ground black pepper
¼ cup all-purpose flour
2 tablespoons olive oil
3 large garlic cloves, crushed
¾ cup dry white wine
2 cups quartered large white mushrooms
1 teaspoon dried marjoram
½ teaspoon dried chervil
1 14½-ounce can Italian plum tomatoes
⅓ cup chopped fresh parsley
16 flour tortillas, warmed

1. Season the chicken with salt and pepper, then dredge in flour, shaking off excess.

2. Place oil in a large skillet over high heat. When hot, add the chicken and cook 5 to 7 minutes or until golden brown on all sides. Remove the chicken from the skillet and keep warm while making the sauce.

3. Return the skillet to the heat and add the garlic and cook 30 seconds, stirring constantly. Add the wine and reduce heat to medium while scraping any brown bits from the bottom of the pan with a wooden spoon. Add the mushrooms, marjoram, chervil, and tomatoes (with their liquid). Break up the tomatoes with a fork. Cover the pan and simmer 20 minutes.

4. Add the cooked chicken to the skillet and continue cooking 10 minutes longer. Stir in the parsley and spoon into warmed tortillas. Fold up burrito style and serve.

Makes 8 to 10 servings

Chicken Mousse Burrito with Beurre Blanc

Mousse

1½ pounds skinless, boneless chicken breast, cut in small pieces
2 cups heavy cream
1 egg
1 tablespoon each chopped fresh thyme, basil, and parsley
¼ teaspoon cayenne pepper
1 teaspoon salt

Butter Sauce

½ cup Chardonnay wine
¼ cup white wine vinegar
2 tablespoons minced shallots
3 black peppercorns, crushed
½ bay leaf
½ cup (1 stick) butter, cut in small pieces, at room temperature
Salt and ground white pepper to taste

12 flour tortillas
Fresh chives for garnish (optional)

1. Preheat the oven to 350° F.

2. In the bowl of a food processor, process the chicken until smooth. With the processor still running, slowly add the cream and the egg. Blend well. Add the herbs and additional seasonings. Turn the mixture into a bowl and chill in refrigerator while making the sauce.

3. Combine the wine, vinegar, shallots, peppercorns, and bay leaf in a small saucepan over high heat. Cook until almost dry.

4. Using a wire whisk, beat in the butter until melted. Do not boil. Season sauce with salt and ground white pepper, then strain through a fine-meshed sieve. Keep warm.

5. Spoon 2 tablespoons of the mousse mixture into the center of each tortilla. Fold the tortilla and place in a buttered ovenproof dish. Continue this process until all the tortillas are filled. Cover the dish with aluminum foil and bake 15 to 20 minutes or until mousse is fully cooked (juices run clear and tortilla is firm to the touch). Transfer burritos to a plate and serve with the sauce. Garnish with chives, if desired.

Makes 6 servings

Coquilles St.-Jacques Burrito

1 tablespoon olive oil
2 tablespoons butter
1 large garlic clove, minced
2 shallots, minced
2 tablespoons flour
1 cup heavy cream
2 pounds bay scallops
1 cup shredded Gruyère cheese
⅛ teaspoon cayenne pepper
1 teaspoon chopped fresh thyme, or ⅛ teaspoon dried
⅛ teaspoon salt
¼ teaspoon ground white pepper
16 flour tortillas, warmed
½ cup chopped fresh parsley

1. Preheat the broiler.

2. Place oil and 1 tablespoon butter in a large skillet over high heat. When hot, add garlic and shallots. Cook, stirring constantly, 1 to 2 minutes or until shallots start to brown slightly. Stir in the flour and continue to cook, stirring for 3 minutes longer. Slowly whisk in the cream so there are no lumps. Reduce heat to low and cook 5 minutes to remove starchy taste from flour. Set aside.

3. In an ovenproof skillet, melt the remaining tablespoon butter over high heat. When hot, add scallops and cook, stirring, 1 to 2 minutes or until opaque. Remove from heat and stir cream mixture into scallops; mix until well blended. Stir in the cheese, cayenne, thyme, salt, and white pepper.

4. Place skillet under broiler and broil for 3 to 5 minutes or until top is a nice golden brown. Remove from oven and let sit for several minutes.

5. Spoon scallop mixture into warmed tortillas, sprinkle generously with parsley, and fold up burrito style.

Makes 8 servings

Salade Niçoise Burrito

Salad

2 tablespoons olive oil
1½ pounds fresh tuna, cut 1 inch thick
1 head Boston lettuce, leaves separated but left whole
3 or 4 anchovy fillets, chopped
1 red bell pepper, cored, seeded, and chopped
1 yellow bell pepper, cored, seeded, and chopped (optional)
4 small plum tomatoes, quartered
3 hard-boiled eggs, sliced
¼ pound haricots verts or thin green beans, trimmed and steamed
1 Kirby cucumber, thinly sliced
1 small red onion, thinly sliced
½ cup Niçoise olives, pitted
½ pound red potatoes, cooked and cut in small cubes

Dressing

1 teaspoon Dijon mustard
1 large garlic clove, minced
½ teaspoon Herbes de Provence (see Note page 56)
2 tablespoons balsamic vinegar
2 teaspoons capers, chopped
¼ cup extra-virgin olive oil

16 flour tortillas, warmed

1. Place oil in a large skillet over high heat. When hot, add the tuna and cook 3 to 5 minutes on each side or until medium-rare. Transfer to a plate and let cool to room temperature. Cut into bite-size pieces and place in a salad bowl along with the other salad ingredients.

2. Combine all the dressing ingredients except the oil in the bowl of a food processor or blender. With the motor running, add the oil in a thin stream until well blended. Pour dressing over salad and toss gently to coat. Spoon into warmed tortillas and fold burrito style.

Makes 8 servings

Note: Herbes de Provence is a combination of thyme, basil, anise seeds, and lavender flowers. It is a wonderful flavoring for salad dressings or meat, poultry, and fish dishes without adding salt.

Bresse-style Chicken Burrito

2 pounds skinless, boneless chicken breasts, cut in ½-inch strips
⅓ cup all-purpose flour
1 tablespoon butter
3 tablespoons vegetable oil
2 large shallots, minced
1 large garlic clove, minced
⅓ cup Madeira wine
1 13¾-ounce can chicken broth
2 medium carrots, peeled, trimmed, and cut in small cubes
1 large potato, peeled and cut in 1-inch cubes
2 celery stalks, cut in 1-inch cubes
2 tablespoons chopped fresh parsley
½ teaspoon salt
¼ teaspoon freshly ground black pepper
16 flour tortillas, warmed

1. Preheat the oven to 300° F.

2. Dredge the chicken in the flour, shaking off any excess. Place the butter and 2 tablespoons oil in a large skillet over high heat. When hot, add the chicken pieces in a single layer and cook 3 to 5 minutes or until golden brown on all sides. Remove chicken with a slotted spoon to a plate. Keep warm.

3. Return the skillet to the heat and add the remaining tablespoon of oil. When hot, add the shallots and garlic and cook, stirring constantly, 3 to 5 minutes or until slightly browned. Add the Madeira, scraping up brown bits from the bottom of the pan. Add broth and vegetables. Reduce heat, cover, and cook 25 to 30 minutes or until vegetables are tender. Add reserved chicken and the parsley and season with salt and pepper. Spoon into warmed tortillas and fold burrito style.

Makes 8 servings

Pear Soufflé Burrito

Poached Pear Puree

2 pounds ripe pears, peeled and cored
2 cups granulated sugar
2 cups water
2 tablespoons fresh lemon juice
¼ cup pear liqueur
3 egg yolks

Pastry Cream

2 cups milk
½ vanilla bean (see Note), or 1 teaspoon vanilla extract
¼ cup plus 2 teaspoons granulated sugar
4 eggs, separated
¼ cup all-purpose flour

8 flour tortillas
Confectioners' sugar

1. In a medium saucepan, combine the pears with the granulated sugar, water, and lemon juice. Cover and cook over high heat 12 to 15 minutes or until very tender. Remove the pears from the poaching liquid and puree in a food processor or blender. Return puree to pan and cook 10 to 15 minutes or until very thick. Cool to room temperature. Add liqueur and yolks and set aside.

2. To make the pastry cream, put the milk in a medium saucepan and scrape vanilla seeds into pan. Add ¼ cup granulated sugar. Cook over medium-high heat until the milk has scalded. Remove from heat.

3. Preheat the oven to 425° F.

4. In a medium mixing bowl, combine the egg yolks and flour and mix well with a wire whisk. Slowly in a thin stream, whisk in the scalded milk until smooth. Place this bowl over a pot of simmering water and cook 15 to 20 minutes or until thickened. Fold the pureed pears into the thickened pastry cream.

5. In another bowl, whisk the egg whites, adding the remaining sugar 1 teaspoon at a time until stiff peaks are formed. Gently fold this into the pastry cream.

6. Divide the soufflé mixture equally among the tortillas, then fold tortillas in half. Place in a buttered baking dish large enough to hold the tortillas in a single layer. Bake 6 to 8 minutes or until puffed. Sprinkle with confectioners' sugar and serve.

Makes 6 servings

Note: Vanilla beans are the seed pod of an orchid plant. They range in quality and price, and are rather expensive, but once you use them for flavoring you won't want to use anything else.

Make an incision along the entire length of the vanilla bean, then scrape out the black seeds inside and add them to the recipe as you would an extract. Vanilla beans are concentrated in flavor; half a bean is enough for this recipe. Not only can you use the seeds inside the bean but you can also steep the bean pod in hot liquid to extract more flavor.

6

Greece

Eggplant, lamb, lemon, and fresh oregano are familiar ingredients found in Greek foods. It seems only natural that the tortilla—similar in shape to the pita—would serve to complement the cuisine of this Mediterranean country.

Taramasalata Burrito

½ cup salmon caviar
2 tablespoons fresh lemon juice
8 ounces French bread slices, soaked in ½ cup water for 10 minutes then squeezed dry
1 large garlic clove, minced
1 tablespoon chopped onion
2 tablespoons chopped fresh parsley
⅛ teaspoon ground white pepper
½ cup extra-virgin olive oil

Salt and freshly ground black pepper to taste
16 flour tortillas, cut in half

1. Preheat the oven to 350° F.

2. Place the first 7 ingredients in the bowl of a food processor fitted with a metal blade or in a blender. Blend on high until a smooth paste forms.

3. With the motor running, slowly add the olive oil in a thin stream until well blended. Season with salt and ground black pepper. Transfer mixture to a small bowl.

4. Spread the taramasalata on the tortillas. Roll up burrito style and place seam side down on a cookie sheet. Bake 5 minutes or until heated through and lightly golden.

5. To serve these burritos as an hors d'oeuvre, cut each in half on an angle.

Makes 6 servings

Spanakopita Burrito Appetizer

2 tablespoons olive oil
1 medium onion, finely minced
4 large garlic cloves, minced
1 10-ounce package frozen chopped spinach, thawed and squeezed dry
1 cup feta cheese, pot cheese, or farmer cheese
⅛ teaspoon ground nutmeg
¼ teaspoon cayenne pepper
2 eggs
½ cup fresh bread crumbs (see Note)
½ cup grated Parmesan cheese
Salt and freshly ground black pepper to taste
12 flour tortillas, cut in three or four 1½-inch strips
4 tablespoons (½ stick) butter, melted

1. Preheat the oven to 350° F.

2. Place oil in a medium skillet over high heat. When hot, add the onion and cook 3 to 5 minutes or until transparent. Add the garlic and cook 1 minute longer. Remove from heat and cool slightly. Add the spinach and cheese and blend well.

3. Stir in the nutmeg, cayenne, eggs, bread crumbs, and Parmesan. Mix well and adjust seasonings with salt and black pepper. Set aside.

4. Line a 12 × 16-inch sheet pan with aluminum foil. Brush the tortilla strips on both sides with melted butter. Spoon a heaping tablespoon of the spinach-cheese mixture onto a tortilla strip and roll up. Place the roll in the pan and continue until all the tortilla strips are used. Bake for 15 to 20 minutes or until golden brown on the edges and heated through.

Makes about 36 pieces

Note: Make your own bread crumbs with any fresh or stale bread you have on hand. Place the pieces in a food processor and process until fine bread crumbs are made.

Fish Burrito with Greek Olives and Roasted Fennel

1½ to 2 pounds white fish fillets, such as cod, halibut, or snapper,
  cut in bite-size pieces
¼ cup all-purpose flour
¼ cup olive oil
1 large onion, thinly sliced
2 large garlic cloves, finely minced
1 fennel bulb, cut in julienne strips (see Note)
½ pound Greek olives, pitted and minced
2 tablespoons anise-flavored liqueur, such as Ouzo
¾ cup chicken broth
1 teaspoon chopped fresh tarragon
Salt and freshly ground black pepper to taste
12 to 16 flour tortillas, warmed

1. Lightly dredge the fish fillets in flour, shaking off excess. Place 2 tablespoons oil in a large skillet over medium-high heat. When oil is hot, add fish in a single layer, cooking in several batches if necessary. Cook 2 to 3 minutes on each side or until golden brown. Remove from pan and keep warm.

2. Add remaining oil to the skillet. When hot, add the onion and cook about 10 minutes or until onion begins to brown slightly. Add the garlic and cook 1 minute longer.

3. Stir in the fennel and olives. Continue to cook 5 to 7 minutes or until fennel is slightly soft. Add liqueur and cook until almost dry. Add the chicken broth, bring to a boil, then reduce heat to low, and simmer 7 to 10 minutes.

4. Remove skillet from heat, add cooked fish, and top with tarragon. Season with salt and pepper. Put in warmed tortillas, fold burrito style, and serve.

Makes 6 to 8 servings

Note: Fennel is a wonderful root vegetable with the lovely fresh flavor of anise. When preparing the fennel, sprinkle a little lemon juice on the slices to keep them from turning brown.

Greek Salad Burrito

Salad

1 head romaine lettuce, trimmed
1 cup Greek olives, pitted and cut in half
1 green bell pepper, cored, seeded, and thinly sliced into rings
1 small red onion, thinly sliced
6 anchovy fillets, chopped
1 cup feta cheese, in small pieces
4 plum tomatoes, diced

Dressing

2 tablespoons fresh lemon juice
¼ cup olive oil
1 tablespoon fresh oregano, or ½ teaspoon dried
¼ teaspoon salt
3 large garlic cloves, crushed

16 flour tortillas, warmed

1. Make the salad by thinly shredding the romaine lettuce and placing it in a large salad bowl. Toss in the olives, green pepper, red onion, anchovies, feta, and tomatoes.

2. Combine the ingredients for the dressing in a small bowl and blend well. Add to the salad and toss gently to coat. Serve salad in warmed tortillas, rolled burrito style.

Makes 8 servings

Lamb Burrito with Avgolemono Sauce

Lamb

1½ pounds boneless leg of lamb, cut in ½-inch cubes
¼ cup chopped fresh oregano, or 1 tablespoon dried
1 teaspoon freshly ground black pepper
½ teaspoon salt
2 tablespoons olive oil
4 large garlic cloves, crushed

Avgolemono Sauce

1 cup chicken broth
3 egg yolks, lightly beaten
¼ cup fresh lemon juice
Salt and freshly ground pepper to taste

16 flour tortillas, warmed

1. Preheat the oven to 425° F.

2. Season the lamb with oregano, pepper, salt, olive oil, and garlic. Roast for 15 to 20 minutes or until medium-rare or desired doneness.

3. Meanwhile, heat the broth in a small saucepan over high heat until simmering. In a separate small bowl, mix the egg yolks and lemon juice. Slowly whisk ¼ cup of the hot broth into the eggs, then stir this mixture back into the broth. (This is called tempering; it allows you to add eggs to a hot liquid without their scrambling.) Continue to cook sauce over medium heat, stirring constantly, until slightly thickened. Do not allow sauce to boil or eggs will scramble. Adjust seasonings with salt and pepper.

4. Spread the lamb on the warmed tortillas and spoon some of the sauce on top. Roll up burrito style and serve immediately.

Makes 8 servings

Scordalia Burrito

2 large potatoes, peeled
12 to 15 garlic cloves, peeled
½ cup olive oil
1 teaspoon salt
¼ teaspoon freshly ground black pepper
¼ cup chopped fresh parsley
1 10-ounce package frozen large lima beans, thawed
12 flour tortillas, warmed

1. Place potatoes in a medium saucepan and enough cold water to cover. Cook over high heat about 30 minutes or until potatoes are very tender. Ten minutes before potatoes are done, add the garlic.

2. Strain the potatoes and garlic in a colander. Using a food mill or electric mixer, mash the potatoes until smooth and the garlic is well blended. Stir in the olive oil, salt, pepper, parsley, and lima beans. Place back in saucepan and reheat over low heat, stirring constantly, until mixture is warm.

3. Spread the potato mixture on warmed tortillas, roll up burrito style, and serve immediately.

Makes 6 servings

Baklava Burrito

Filling

½ pound sliced almonds, toasted
¼ cup sugar
1 teaspoon ground cinnamon
⅛ teaspoon ground cloves

6 8-inch flour tortillas
½ cup (1 stick) butter, melted

Syrup

1 cup honey
1 cup sugar
1 cup water
2 tablespoons fresh lemon juice
1 cinnamon stick
1 whole clove

1. Preheat the oven to 350° F.

2. In the bowl of a food processor fitted with a metal blade, process the almonds, sugar, cinnamon, and cloves until finely chopped.

3. Place 1 tortilla in an 8-inch pie plate and brush the surface with butter. Sprinkle some of the nut mixture on top. Place another tortilla on top of this and brush with butter again. Repeat this procedure until all the tortillas and filling are used, ending with a tortilla on the top. Pour any remaining butter over top and bake for 10 minutes. Reduce heat to 300° F. and continue baking 15 to 20 minutes longer or until top starts to brown.

4. While the baklava bakes, prepare the syrup. Place the syrup ingredients in a small saucepan and bring to a boil over high heat. Reduce heat to medium and continue to cook slowly for 20 minutes or until the syrup is thickened, reduced by half, and coats the back of a spoon.

5. Remove the baklava from the oven and strain the syrup through a wire-mesh sieve over the top. Allow it to cool to room temperature, then cut into wedges. Spoon extra syrup over each portion.

Makes 6 to 8 servings

7

China

Because of its similarity to the Chinese pancake, the flour tortilla is a natural fit with classic Chinese food. When you try the Egg Roll Burrito and the Moo Shu Vegetable Burrito, you will be delighted by the similarity and intrigued by the tortilla's ability to adapt.

Chinese Shrimp-Toast Burrito Appetizer

½ pound cooked shrimp, chopped
1 tablespoon finely minced bacon
2 tablespoons minced onion
3 tablespoons minced fresh ginger
1 tablespoon minced green onion
1 tablespoon teriyaki sauce
1 tablespoon cornstarch
1 egg
½ teaspoon salt
½ teaspoon sugar
⅔ cup fresh bread crumbs (see Note page 64)
2 cups vegetable oil for frying
Four 8-inch tortillas, each cut in 8 triangles

1. In a small bowl, combine the shrimp, bacon, onion, ginger, green onion, teriyaki sauce, cornstarch, egg, salt, and sugar.

2. Heat the oil in a wok or high-sided skillet until it registers 350° F. on a deep-fat frying thermometer. Place ½ tablespoon of the shrimp mixture on each tortilla triangle. Press fresh bread crumbs onto the surface and roll up, starting with the pointed end first. Skewer with a toothpick or hold in place with tongs while frying.

3. Cook 1 to 2 minutes or until golden brown on all sides. Drain on paper towels and serve with additional teriyaki sauce, if desired.

Makes 32 mini-burritos

Egg Roll Burrito

2 tablespoons vegetable oil
½ pound boneless pork loin, cut in thin strips
1 small onion, finely minced
2 celery stalks, chopped
1 medium carrot, peeled and chopped
1 tablespoon grated fresh ginger
1 large garlic clove, minced
¼ cup reduced-sodium soy sauce
1 teaspoon sugar
2 cups mung bean sprouts
1 cup chopped fresh spinach leaves
6 flour tortillas
Vegetable oil for frying
Hot Chinese-style mustard (optional)
Sweet and Sour Sauce (optional; recipe follows)

1. Place 1 tablespoon vegetable oil in a large skillet over high heat. When hot, add the pork and cook, stirring constantly, 3 to 5 minutes or until just cooked through. Transfer the pork to a large mixing bowl. Add remaining tablespoon of oil to the same skillet over high heat. When hot, add the onion, celery, and carrot. Cook 3 minutes or until vegetables are tender. Stir in the ginger and garlic; cook 1 to 2 minutes longer.

2. Reduce heat to medium. Stir in the soy sauce and sugar. Add the bean sprouts and cook 5 minutes or until the sprouts are slightly wilted but still crunchy. Remove from heat and stir in spinach leaves.

3. Allow the vegetable mixture to cool completely, then add to the pork. Mix well.

4. Spoon about 2 tablespoons of the pork filling in the center of a flour tortilla. Fold in sides to ½ inch, then roll the tortilla up lengthwise. Secure each tortilla with a wooden toothpick.

5. Pour 2 inches of vegetable oil in a large saucepan with high sides. Heat over high heat; when the temperature has reached 350° F. on a deep-fat frying thermometer, fry the rolls, one at a time and holding with metal tongs, about 3 minutes or until golden brown on all sides. Drain the cooked rolls on a plate lined with paper towels. Remove toothpicks and keep rolls warm in oven while frying remaining ones. Serve with hot mustard and sauce, if desired.

Makes 6 servings

Sweet and Sour Sauce

¼ **cup fresh orange juice**
2 **tablespoons fresh lemon juice**
2 **tablespoons coarsely chopped fresh ginger**
½ **cup ketchup**
2 **tablespoons brown sugar**
2 **tablespoons hoisin sauce**
½ **teaspoon Asian sesame oil**
½ **cup sugar**
¼ **cup rice wine vinegar**

Combine all the ingredients in a saucepan and bring to a boil over high heat. Reduce heat to low and simmer 5 minutes. Remove from heat and cool completely.

Makes about 1½ cups

Oriental Steamed-Bass Burrito

2 pounds sea bass fillet, cut in 1-inch chunks
½ cup dry white wine
2 tablespoons rice wine vinegar
2 tablespoons peanut oil
2 small garlic cloves, minced
¼ cup chopped fresh ginger
1 bunch green onions, thinly sliced; plus 2 green onions, cut in 1-inch julienne
    pieces for garnish (optional)
⅓ cup reduced-sodium soy sauce
1 tablespoon sugar
2 teaspoons Asian sesame oil
12 flour tortillas, warmed

1. Preheat oven to 350° F.

2. Place the fish in a shallow casserole dish. Sprinkle with the wine, vinegar, oil, garlic, ginger, and sliced green onions. Cover and steam 5 to 7 minutes or until opaque.

3. Combine the soy sauce and sugar in a small saucepan over medium heat. Bring to a boil, turn off heat, and add sesame oil.

4. Remove cooked fish from oven and spread soy sauce mixture over top. Place immediately in warmed tortillas, roll burrito style, and garnish with julienned green onion, if desired.

Makes 6 servings

Shrimp with Black Bean and Broccoli Burrito

½ cup vegetable oil
1½ pounds medium shrimp, peeled and deveined (see Note page 46)
2 tablespoons finely chopped fresh ginger
1 large garlic clove, minced
2 tablespoons salted black beans, rinsed (see Note)
1 large red bell pepper, cored, seeded, and chopped
1 head broccoli, trimmed and cut in flowerettes
¼ cup reduced-sodium soy sauce
2 tablespoons dry sherry
1 teaspoon sugar
1 tablespoon cornstarch, dissolved in 2 tablespoons cold water
Salt and freshly ground black pepper to taste
½ cup minced green onions
16 flour tortillas, warmed

1. Place oil in a wok or high-sided skillet over high heat. When hot, add the shrimp and cook 3 minutes or until pink. Remove shrimp from pan with slotted spoon and keep warm on platter. Discard all but 2 tablespoons oil. Return pan to heat.

2. Add the ginger, garlic, black beans, red pepper, and broccoli to the wok or skillet. Stir-fry for 1 minute, then add shrimp. Season with soy sauce, sherry, sugar, and cornstarch mixture. Cook 1 minute or until slightly thickened. Adjust seasonings with salt and pepper. Remove from heat and stir in minced green onions. Place in warmed tortillas and roll up burrito style. Serve.

Makes 8 servings

Note: Salted black beans can be found in most Asian markets and many supermarkets.

Roast Pork Burrito with Sticky Rice

Marinade

2 large garlic cloves, crushed
2 tablespoons honey
½ cup dark soy sauce
¼ cup dry sherry
2 tablespoons fresh lemon juice
1 cup vegetable oil
½ cup minced green onions
1 pork tenderloin, about 1 pound, trimmed

Rice

1 cup short-grain, glutinous rice
1 cup water
2 tablespoons rice wine vinegar

16 flour tortillas, warmed
½ cup chopped green onions (optional)

1. In a large ceramic or glass bowl, combine the garlic, honey, soy sauce, sherry, lemon juice, oil, and green onions. Add the pork and marinate 6 hours or overnight.

2. Drain pork. Preheat the broiler or prepare a charcoal grill. When hot, cook pork on all sides 10 to 15 minutes or until medium-rare or desired doneness. Cut pork in thin slices. Set aside.

3. Cook the rice using a Chinese steamer or by combining the rice and water in a small saucepan over high heat. When it begins to boil, cover the pan and reduce heat to low and simmer about 10 minutes. Then turn off heat and leave until all the water has been absorbed. Sprinkle with rice wine vinegar and fluff gently with a fork.

4. To serve, layer a small amount of sticky rice in the center of each warmed tortilla. Top with several slices of the pork and wrap burrito style. Garnish with green onions, if desired.

Makes 8 servings

Moo Shu Vegetable Burrito

2 tablespoons vegetable oil
1 large garlic clove, minced
3 tablespoons chopped fresh ginger
1 pound mung bean sprouts
¼ pound snow peas, trimmed and cut in half
2 celery stalks, peeled and chopped
2 medium carrots, peeled and chopped
1 8-ounce can whole water chestnuts, drained and diced
2 teaspoons Asian sesame oil
1 tablespoon reduced-sodium soy sauce
1 cup plum sauce (see Note)
12 flour tortillas, warmed

1. Place oil in a medium skillet over high heat. When hot, add the garlic and ginger. Cook, stirring constantly, 1 to 2 minutes.

2. Add the vegetables and cook, stirring, about 5 minutes or until crisp-tender. Remove from heat. Stir in sesame oil and soy sauce. Spoon into warmed tortillas and top with plum sauce. Roll up burrito style and serve.

Makes 6 servings

Note: Plum sauce can be found in most supermarkets.

Szechuan Beef Burrito

Marinade

¼ cup reduced-sodium soy sauce
2 tablespoons crushed Szechuan peppercorns (see Note), or ¼ cup crushed hot
    red pepper flakes
1 egg white
1 tablespoon cornstarch
2 cups plus 1 tablespoon vegetable oil
1½ pounds flank steak, trimmed and cut against the grain in ½-inch-thick slices

Sauce

¼ cup reduced-sodium soy sauce
½ cup chicken broth
1 tablespoon rice wine vinegar
1 tablespoon sugar
3 tablespoons minced fresh ginger
2 medium garlic cloves, minced
1 tablespoon hot chili oil
1 teaspoon Asian sesame oil

16 flour tortillas, warmed
5 green onions, cut in 1-inch julienne strips
2 cups finely shredded Savoy cabbage

1. In a large mixing bowl, combine the soy sauce, peppercorns or flakes, egg white, cornstarch, and 1 tablespoon vegetable oil. Add the steak and toss to coat. Marinate for 1 hour.

2. Heat 2 cups vegetable oil in a wok or high-sided skillet over high heat until it reaches 350° F. on a deep-fat frying thermometer. Drain the steak and add to the hot oil. Cook about 1 minute or until golden brown. Using a slotted spoon, transfer meat to a platter and keep warm.

3. In a small bowl, combine the sauce ingredients. Pour over cooked meat and toss well. Serve in warmed tortillas with green onions and cabbage. Roll up burrito style and serve.

Makes 8 servings

Note: Szechuan peppercorns can be found in most supermarkets and in Asian markets.

Sweet Red Bean Burrito

10 ounces Asian red beans such as azuki or red mung (see Note)
1 1-inch chunk of fresh ginger, peeled
½ cup packed dark brown sugar
2 tablespoons soybean paste
12 flour tortillas

1. Soak the beans overnight in enough water to cover. Drain and place beans in a saucepot fitted with a lid and cover with cold water. Bring to a boil over high heat, reduce heat to medium, and simmer 1 hour, adding more water as needed or until beans are tender.

2. Preheat the oven to 400° F.

3. When beans are tender, drain and place in food processor or blender along with remaining ingredients and process to a smooth paste. Thin with 2 tablespoons to ¼ cup water if paste is too thick.

4. Spoon the bean paste into the tortillas, roll up and place on a cookie sheet. Loosely cover the burritos with aluminum foil. Bake about 10 minutes or until thoroughly heated.

Makes 6 servings

Note: Asian red beans can be found in most specialty food stores and Asian groceries. You may also substitute cooked red kidney beans if necessary.

8

Hungary

Although Hungary is far from the countries whose bread needs are met principally by the tortilla, the hearty and wholesome food that is Hungarian makes great burrito fillings.

Tokany of Veal Burrito

3 tablespoons vegetable oil
2 tablespoons butter
½ cup all-purpose flour
1½ pounds boneless veal shoulder, cut in ½-inch cubes
3 large onions, thinly sliced
1 cup dry white wine, such as Chablis
1 green bell pepper, cored, seeded, and chopped
2 medium carrots, peeled and chopped
1 large tomato, chopped
2 tablespoons sweet Hungarian paprika (see Note 1 page 86)
½ cup beef broth
1 pound white mushrooms
½ cup sour cream or crème fraîche (see Note 2 page 86)
2 tablespoons chopped fresh parsley
Salt and pepper to taste
16 flour tortillas, warmed

1. In a large casserole fitted with a lid, heat the oil and butter over high heat until the butter has melted and it begins to brown.

2. Flour the veal, shaking off any excess. Add in a single layer to the casserole and cook 7 to 10 minutes or until golden brown on all sides. Remove meat with a slotted spoon and set aside.

3. Add the onions to the casserole. Cook about 10 minutes or until the onions start to turn brown and caramelize. Add the wine and, using a wooden spoon, scrape any brown bits from the bottom of the pan. Add the green pepper, carrots, tomato, paprika, broth, and veal. Cover and simmer 45 to 50 minutes or until veal is extremely tender. Ten minutes before veal is done, uncover the casserole and add the mushrooms. Remove from the heat and stir in the sour cream. Sprinkle with parsley and season with salt and pepper.

4. Spoon veal mixture into the tortillas, roll up burrito style, and serve immediately.

Makes 8 servings

Note 1: Paprika is a prized spice in Hungary, although it is used as a food coloring agent in many other cuisines. It has a unique and distinctive flavor, and comes in both sweet and hot varieties.

Note 2: Make your own crème fraîche by combining 2 cups heavy cream with 2 tablespoons buttermilk. Place in a glass container and cover tightly with plastic wrap. Let stand in a warm place for 12 hours or until slightly thicker than heavy cream, then refrigerate.

Hungarian-Style Crab Salad Burrito

Salad

1 pound fresh crab meat, picked over for shells and cartilage
1 small onion, finely minced
1 green bell pepper, cored, seeded, and finely chopped
1 celery stalk, finely chopped
2 hard-boiled eggs, chopped

Dressing

2 tablespoons white wine vinegar
2 teaspoons sweet Hungarian paprika (see Note 1 page 86)
1 large garlic clove, minced
¼ teaspoon black pepper
1 teaspoon dry mustard
½ cup vegetable oil
Salt to taste

Bibb lettuce leaves
12 flour tortillas, warmed

1. In a large mixing bowl, combine the crab, onion, green pepper, celery, and chopped egg.

2. In another small bowl, combine the vinegar, paprika, garlic, pepper, and mustard and whisk together. Using a wire whisk, slowly, add the oil in a thin stream until well incorporated. Season with salt.

3. Pour dressing over the crab salad and toss to coat. Let stand at room temperature 20 minutes before serving.

4. Place lettuce leaves on tortillas and spoon crab salad on top. Roll up burrito style and serve immediately.

Makes 6 servings

Chicken Paprikash Burrito

2 tablespoons vegetable oil
1 tablespoon butter
2 pounds skinless, boneless chicken, dark and light meat, cut in ½-inch chunks
1 large onion, chopped
¼ cup sweet Hungarian paprika (see Note 1 page 86)
¼ teaspoon salt
1 cup water
1 green bell pepper, cored, seeded, and cut in ¼-inch cubes
1 medium tomato, diced
1 teaspoon tomato paste
½ cup sour cream or plain yogurt
1 cup cooked white rice (optional)
16 to 20 flour tortillas, warmed

1. Place oil and butter in a medium skillet over high heat. When hot, add the chicken in a single layer and cook 7 to 10 minutes or until golden brown. Add onion and paprika. Cook, stirring, 3 to 5 minutes or until onion is soft. Add salt, water, green pepper, tomato, and tomato paste. Stir well.

2. Reduce heat to low. Cover and simmer 40 minutes or until chicken is very tender. Remove pan from heat and stir in sour cream or yogurt.

3. Spoon paprikash over rice, if desired, and then into warmed tortillas. Fold burrito style and serve.

Makes 8 to 10 servings

Hungarian Lamb and Spinach Burrito

1½ pounds boneless lamb shank, cut in ½-inch chunks
¼ cup all-purpose flour
¼ cup vegetable oil
1 large onion, thinly sliced
2 teaspoons hot Hungarian paprika (see Note 1 page 86)
2 10-ounce packages frozen chopped spinach, thawed and squeezed dry
½ cup beef broth
½ cup ricotta or pot cheese
1 cup sour cream
Salt and pepper to taste
16 flour tortillas, warmed

1. Dredge the meat in the flour, shaking off any excess. Put oil in a large casserole over high heat. When hot, add the lamb and cook 5 to 7 minutes or until golden brown on all sides. Remove the seared lamb from the pan and set aside.

2. Add the onion and cook 7 to 10 minutes or until onion starts to brown. Add paprika and cook 3 to 5 minutes longer. Strain any excess fat from the casserole.

3. Add spinach and lamb. Stir in broth, cover, and reduce heat to medium. Simmer 45 minutes to 1 hour or until meat is quite tender and spinach is very soft.

4. Stir in cheese and sour cream. Cook until just heated through. Do not allow stew to boil. Season with salt and pepper, then spoon into warmed tortillas and roll up burrito style.

Makes 8 servings

Beef Goulash Burrito

3 tablespoons butter
3 small onions, finely minced
3 small garlic cloves, minced
1 teaspoon dried marjoram
1½ pounds lean ground beef
3 tablespoons hot Hungarian paprika (see Note 1 page 86)
¼ cup tomato paste
1½ cups beef broth
1 bay leaf
2 cups cooked egg noodles (optional)
16 flour tortillas, warmed

1. Place butter in a large skillet over high heat. When hot, add the onions and cook, stirring constantly, for 3 to 5 minutes or until onions are transparent. Add the garlic and cook 1 to 2 minutes longer. Add the marjoram and ground beef, breaking up the beef with a fork as it cooks.

2. When the meat has browned, carefully drain off any excess fat. Return the pan to the heat. Add the paprika, tomato paste, broth, and bay leaf. Bring to a boil, reduce heat to low, and simmer 20 minutes or until sauce is slightly thickened. Remove bay leaf.

3. Spoon noodles, if using, into warmed tortillas, then top with the goulash and fold into burritos.

Makes 8 servings

Steak Burrito with Sour Cream–Caper Sauce

1 pound boneless sirloin steak, cut in ¼-inch-thin strips
1 medium onion, thinly sliced
2 red bell peppers, cored, seeded, and cut in julienne strips
1 large garlic clove, minced
3 tablespoons capers
½ cup sweet dessert wine
¼ cup heavy cream
½ cup sour cream
½ teaspoon freshly ground black pepper
¼ teaspoon salt
12 flour tortillas, warmed

1. Place oil in a large skillet over high heat. When hot, add steak and cook 2 to 3 minutes or until just browned but still rare. Transfer to plate and set aside.

2. Add onion and red peppers. Cook, stirring constantly, 3 to 5 minutes or until soft. Add the garlic and capers and cook 30 seconds longer. Stir in wine. Using a wooden spoon, scrape any brown bits from the bottom of the pan, and cook until the wine is reduced by half. Stir in the cream and reduce 5 minutes until it coats the back of a spoon.

3. Remove skillet from the heat and stir in the sour cream. Season with pepper and salt. Add steak strips and any juices, then toss to coat. Serve in warmed flour tortillas and fold into burritos.

Makes 6 servings

Palascinta Burrito

Pancakes

½ **cup heavy cream**
½ **cup ground walnuts**
½ **cup ground pecans**
⅓ **cup confectioners' sugar**
½ **cup chopped golden raisins**
Grated rind from 1 orange
½ **cup (1 stick) butter, melted**
8 to 10 flour tortillas

Sauce

1 cup semisweet chocolate chips
1 tablespoon superfine sugar
2 tablespoons white rum

1 pint fresh raspberries (optional)

1. Preheat the oven to 400° F.

2. In a medium saucepan, combine the cream, nuts, confectioners' sugar, raisins, orange rind, and half the butter and bring to a simmer over low heat. Cook 5 to 7 minutes or until the mixture thickens. Remove from heat. Spoon 1 to 1½ tablespoons mixture into the center of each tortilla. Gently fold in half and then in half again to form a triangle.

3. Place the remaining butter in a large skillet. When hot, cook the tortilla pancakes 2 to 3 minutes on each side or until golden brown on both sides. Transfer to a baking dish, cover, and bake for about 5 minutes or until hot.

4. Heat the chocolate with the sugar and rum in a double boiler until just melted (see Note). Spoon sauce over pancakes and serve with fresh raspberries, if desired.

Makes 8 to 10 servings

Note: Melting chocolate can be tricky. Chocolate melts at 90° F. but scalds at 120° F. Heat a pot of water to just simmering. Turn off the heat and place a bowl with the chocolate, sugar, and rum over the top. By adding a liquid along with the chocolate, you help stabilize it and keep it from getting grainy. Make certain you stir the mixture often until it just melts. Be careful that the bottom of the bowl is not touching the surface of the water, since this might cause the chocolate to burn.

9

Spain

The cuisine of Spain uses a number of ingredients familiar to and loved by all. Among these are olive oil, tomatoes, garlic, basil, sherry, and chorizo. When united with the flour tortilla, Spanish food makes outstanding burritos.

Salmon with Sherry and Aïoli Burrito

Fish

1½ pounds salmon fillet, cut in ½-inch chunks
2 tablespoons flour
2 tablespoons vegetable oil
2 tablespoons minced shallots
¼ cup dry sherry
½ cup chicken broth
2 tablespoons chopped fresh parsley

Aïoli

1 cup mayonnaise
3 small garlic cloves, crushed
2 teaspoons chopped capers
2 tablespoons olive oil
1 teaspoon coarsely ground black pepper
1 tablespoon chopped fresh parsley
1 tablespoon chopped fresh basil

12 flour tortillas, warmed

1. Dredge the salmon in the flour, shaking off excess. Place the oil in a large skillet over high heat. When hot, add the salmon and cook 3 to 5 minutes or until golden brown. Add the shallots and cook 2 to 3 minutes longer. Stir in the sherry and chicken broth, and reduce the sauce by half. Remove from heat and keep warm. Sprinkle with chopped parsley.

2. Combine the ingredients for the aïoli in a small bowl. Let sit at room temperature for 20 minutes so flavors can develop.

3. Put salmon in warmed tortillas and top with sauce. Fold as for burritos, and serve.

Makes 6 servings

Paella Burrito

¼ cup olive oil
½ pound medium shrimp, peeled and deveined (see Note page 46)
½ pound skinless, boneless chicken thigh meat, cut in ½-inch pieces
1 medium onion, chopped
3 large garlic cloves, minced
1 green bell pepper, cored, seeded, and chopped
½ pound chorizo or sweet Italian sausage, removed from casings
1 cup white rice
2½ cups clam or chicken broth
¼ teaspoon saffron threads
1 8-ounce can chopped clams, with juice
1 cup fresh or frozen peas
¼ cup diced pimientos
½ teaspoon salt (optional)
Freshly ground black pepper to taste
16 to 20 flour tortillas, warmed or grilled

1. Place oil in a large, high-sided skillet or paella pan over high heat. When hot, add the shrimp and cook, stirring constantly, 3 to 5 minutes or until they turn a light pink color. Remove shrimp from pan with slotted spoon and set aside.

2. Add the chicken to the skillet and cook 5 to 7 minutes or until golden brown. Remove chicken from pan and set aside.

3. Return the skillet to the heat and add the onion. Cook, stirring, 1 to 2 minutes or until onion is transparent. Add the garlic and cook 1 minute longer. Stir in the green pepper and sausage. Cook 5 minutes or until the sausage starts to brown. Add the rice and stir to coat with the oil and fat from the sausage. Add the clam or chicken broth and saffron. Bring to a boil. Reduce heat to medium, cover, and simmer 20 to 30 minutes or until all the liquid has been absorbed.

4. Ten minutes before the rice is done, add the shrimp and chicken, the chopped clams with their juice, peas, and pimientos. Season with salt, if necessary, and plenty of ground black pepper.

5. Spoon into the warmed tortillas and fold burrito style.

Makes 8 to 10 servings

Catalán Chicken Picada Burrito

Stew

3 tablespoons olive oil
1½ pounds skinless, boneless chicken, dark and light meat, cut in ½-inch pieces
2 large onions, sliced
4 large carrots, peeled and cut in ¼-inch slices
1 pound white mushrooms, sliced
½ cup chicken broth
½ cup dry white wine
Salt and pepper to taste

Picada

½ cup slivered almonds, toasted
4 large garlic cloves, minced
½ teaspoon saffron threads (optional)
¼ cup chopped fresh parsley

16 flour tortillas, warmed
2 hard-boiled eggs, chopped

1. Place oil in a large skillet over high heat. When hot, add the chicken and cook 3 to 5 minutes or until golden brown. Remove chicken to platter and set aside.

2. Return pan to heat and add onions and carrots. Cook, stirring constantly, until onions become transparent. Add the mushrooms and cook 1 to 2 minutes longer. Then reduce heat to low and stir in the broth and wine. Simmer 3 to 5 minutes. Add chicken to pan and cover. Keep warm.

3. Combine almonds, garlic, saffron, and parsley in the bowl of a food processor fitted with a metal blade. Process until nuts are well chopped.

4. Stir picada into chicken and season with salt and pepper. Spoon into warmed tortillas, sprinkle top with chopped egg, and fold up burrito style.

Makes 8 servings

Basque Chorizo Burrito with Salsa Verde

¼ **cup vegetable oil**
2 **pounds chorizo sausage, cut in bite-size pieces**
4 **large garlic cloves, sliced**
2 **green bell peppers, cored, seeded, and cut in ¼-inch cubes**
¼ **cup chopped fresh basil or parsley**
4 **large tomatillas, chopped**
2 **tablespoons chopped cilantro**
2 **tablespoons sherry vinegar**
1 **teaspoon salt**
¼ **teaspoon ground black pepper**
16 **whole wheat tortillas, warmed**

1. Place the oil in a large skillet over high heat. When hot, add the sausage and cook 5 to 7 minutes or until golden brown on all sides. Remove the sausage with a slotted spoon and set aside.

2. To the same pan add the garlic and green peppers and cook 3 to 5 minutes or until peppers are soft and garlic is fragrant. Add the basil, tomatillas, and cilantro and cook 3 to 5 minutes longer. Remove from the heat and stir in the vinegar, salt, and pepper.

3. Transfer mixture to the bowl of a blender or food processor fitted with a metal blade, and process slightly until the consistency of a chunky sauce. Return sauce to the skillet and cook 7 to 10 minutes over low heat or until it thickens slightly. Stir in the sausage and cook until just heated through.

4. Spoon the sausage mixture into warmed tortillas and roll up burrito style.

Makes 8 servings

Trout with Prosciutto Burrito

8 trout fillets, skinned and boned
Freshly ground white pepper to taste
½ pound prosciutto, thinly sliced
1 cup dry white wine
1 bay leaf
1 lemon, thinly sliced
1 tablespoon chopped fresh thyme, or 1 teaspoon dried
¼ cup chopped fresh parsley
2 tablespoons extra-virgin olive oil
1 large garlic clove, minced
2 bunches arugula, cleaned and destemmed
16 flour tortillas, warmed

1. Preheat the oven to 400° F. Line a broiler pan with aluminum foil.

2. Season the trout with white pepper. Wrap each fillet with several slices of the prosciutto. Place on the broiler pan and pour wine over all. Add bay leaf, lemon, thyme, parsley, oil, and garlic.

3. Bake for 5 to 7 minutes or until fish is opaque and flakes easily.

4. Place the arugula in the center of each warmed tortilla. Top with the trout, fold burrito style, and serve.

Makes 8 servings

Caramelized Oranges Burrito

2 cups sugar
6 seedless oranges, peeled and cut in ¼-inch slices
¼ cup orange juice
¼ cup sweet sherry
6 flour tortillas
2 tablespoons butter, melted
1 quart good-quality vanilla ice cream
2 tablespoons chopped fresh mint

1. Preheat the oven to 400° F.

2. Place the sugar in a large skillet and cook over medium-high heat 5 to 7 minutes or until it reaches a golden caramel color. Remove pan from the heat and stir in the orange slices, juice, and sherry.

3. Brush the tortillas with melted butter. Place on a cookie sheet and bake until lightly browned on the edges.

4. Place tortillas on individual plates. Spoon some orange slices into each tortilla, fold up burrito style, and top with vanilla ice cream. Sprinkle with fresh chopped mint, and serve.

Makes 6 servings

10

United States

Our diverse cuisine uses several ingredients that have become synonymous with American food—corn, tomatoes, pecans, and apples, to mention a few. And with such a strong Latin American influence in the United States, it seems only logical that the tortilla as a burrito would find a home here.

Corn Salad Burrito

2 10-ounce packages frozen corn kernels, thawed and drained
2 red bell peppers, cored, seeded, and chopped
1 green bell pepper, cored, seeded, and chopped
1 small red onion, minced
2 large garlic cloves, minced
¼ cup chopped cilantro
2 tablespoons fresh lime juice (see Note page 32)
1 teaspoon salt
1 jalapeño pepper, seeded and chopped (see Note page 33)
¼ cup corn oil
12 whole wheat tortillas, warmed

1. In a medium bowl, combine all the ingredients except the tortillas. Toss to coat and allow to sit at room temperature for 30 minutes so flavors may develop.

2. Spoon corn salad into warmed tortillas, fold as for burritos, and serve. (This dish should always be served at room temperature.)

Makes 6 servings

California Veggie Burrito

Salad

1 large Haas avocado, peeled, seeded, and cut in ¼-inch chunks (see
   Note page 29)
1 cup chopped cauliflower
1 cup grated carrots
1 cup chopped broccoli
1 small red onion, thinly sliced
2 tablespoons fresh lemon juice
½ cup sun-dried tomatoes in oil, chopped

Dressing

1 cup plain yogurt or sour cream
2 tablespoons crumbled blue cheese
1 teaspoon Worcestershire sauce
3 tablespoons milk
½ teaspoon Dijon mustard
¼ teaspoon ground black pepper
¼ teaspoon dried thyme

1 cup alfalfa sprouts
12 whole wheat tortillas, warmed

1. In a large mixing bowl, combine the avocado, cauliflower, carrots, broccoli, onion, lemon juice, and tomatoes.

2. In the bowl of a food processor fitted with a metal blade, combine the dressing ingredients and blend until smooth. Pour this over the vegetables and toss to coat.

3. Spread some of the alfalfa sprouts in the middle of each of the warmed tortillas. Top with the veggie salad and wrap up burrito style.

Makes 6 servings

Chicken Jambalaya Burrito

1 tablespoon olive oil
1 pound skinless, boneless chicken, cut in ½-inch chunks
1 medium onion, chopped
1 large garlic clove, minced
1 cup diced bacon
1 cup long-grain white rice
1 cup drained canned tomatoes
1 13¾-ounce can chicken broth
1 tablespoon chopped fresh sage, or 1 teaspoon dried
½ teaspoon dried thyme
¼ cup chopped fresh parsley
¼ teaspoon salt
1 teaspoon freshly ground black pepper
16 to 18 flour tortillas, warmed

1. Place oil in a large skillet over high heat. When hot, add chicken pieces and cook 5 to 7 minutes or until chicken starts to brown. Add the onion and cook 3 to 5 minutes longer. Stir in the garlic and bacon. Cook 3 to 5 minutes or until bacon starts to get crisp.

2. Add the rice and stir to coat. Add the tomatoes, broth, sage, and thyme. Bring to a boil, cover, and reduce heat to low. Simmer 15 to 20 minutes or until all the liquid has been absorbed and the rice is tender. Sprinkle with parsley, salt, and pepper and toss gently. Spoon into warmed tortillas, fold burrito style, then serve.

Makes 8 or 9 servings

Louisiana Crab Cake Burrito

Crab Cakes

½ **cup vegetable oil**
1 **large onion, finely chopped**
3 **large garlic cloves, minced**
½ **teaspoon cayenne pepper**
1 **pound crab meat, picked over for shells and cartilage**
½ **cup finely chopped cilantro**

1 **teaspoon salt**
4 **cups fresh bread crumbs (see Note page 64)**
4 **eggs**
½ **cup heavy cream**
Salt and black pepper to taste
½ **cup all-purpose flour**

Tartar Sauce

1 cup mayonnaise
2 tablespoons fresh lemon juice
2 tablespoons chopped fresh dill, or 1 teaspoon dried
1 tablespoon chopped capers
¼ cup chopped cornichons or garlic-dill pickles
1 tablespoon finely minced red onion
¼ teaspoon salt
¼ teaspoon freshly ground black pepper

16 flour tortillas, warmed

1. Place 2 tablespoons oil in a large skillet over high heat. When hot, add the onion and cook 3 to 5 minutes or until transparent. Add the garlic and cook 1 to 2 minutes longer. Add cayenne and cook, stirring constantly, for 1 minute. Remove pan from heat and cool completely. Add the crab meat, cilantro, salt, 2 cups bread crumbs, 2 eggs, and the cream. Adjust seasonings with salt and pepper and mix well.

2. Form the crab mixture into eight 2½-inch-wide and 1-inch-thick cakes. Dip each cake in flour, then in the remaining 2 eggs which have been lightly beaten, then in the remaining 2 cups of bread crumbs. Place the breaded crab cakes on a platter and refrigerate for about 30 minutes.

3. In a separate large skillet, heat the remaining oil over medium-high heat. When hot, add the crab cakes in a single layer, cooking in several batches, if necessary. Cook 3 to 5 minutes on each side or until golden brown and heated through. Keep warm in oven.

4. In a small mixing bowl, combine the tartar sauce ingredients and mix well.

5. Serve half a crab cake in each of the warmed flour tortillas and top with the sauce. Fold burrito style and serve immediately.

Makes 8 servings

Maine Lobster Salad Burrito

Salad

1 pound cooked, shelled lobster meat, diced
2 celery stalks, peeled and cut in small cubes
½ medium red onion, minced
1 tablespoon chopped fresh tarragon, or 1 teaspoon dried
⅛ teaspoon salt, or to taste

Dressing

1 tablespoon tarragon vinegar
½ teaspoon Dijon mustard
1 small garlic clove, minced
¼ cup vegetable oil

2 cups mesclun salad greens, trimmed and washed (see Note)
12 to 16 flour tortillas, warmed
12 cherry tomatoes, quartered

1. In a medium mixing bowl, combine the lobster, celery, onion, tarragon, and salt.

2. In a small bowl or the bowl of a food processor fitted with a metal blade, combine the vinegar, mustard, and garlic. Using a wire whisk or with the processor running, add the oil slowly in a thin stream until thoroughly incorporated and well blended. Toss the dressing with the lobster salad.

3. To serve, place a few leaves of salad greens in the middle of a warmed tortilla. Spoon the lobster salad over and garnish with cherry tomatoes. Roll up burrito style and serve immediately.

Makes 6 to 8 servings

Note: Mesclun is a mixture of seasonal baby greens, offering a diversity of tastes in a single bite. Some of the greens may be baby Bibb, mustard greens, mizuna, baby romaine, baby oak leaf, and fresh herbs.

Oregon Morel Mushroom and Wild Rice Burrito

1 cup wild rice
4 cups water or chicken broth
2 tablespoons butter
1 medium onion, minced
2 large garlic cloves, minced
1 tablespoon chopped fresh rosemary, or 1 teaspoon dried
½ pound morel or Portobello mushrooms, cut in thick slices (if unavailable, additional white mushrooms can be substituted)
1 pound white mushrooms, cut in thick slices
½ cup chicken broth
⅓ cup Madeira or Port
½ cup heavy cream
1 teaspoon salt
½ teaspoon freshly ground black pepper
½ cup minced fresh chives
16 whole wheat tortillas

1. In a small saucepan, combine the wild rice and water or broth and bring to a boil over high heat. Cover, reduce heat to low, and simmer 50 minutes or until rice is tender. Drain any excess broth from rice, if necessary. Set aside.

2. Place butter in a large skillet over high heat. When hot, add the onion and cook for 3 to 5 minutes or until slightly wilted. Add the garlic and rosemary and cook 1 to 2 minutes longer.

3. Stir in the wild and white mushrooms and cook, stirring occasionally, until just soft. Add broth and simmer 15 minutes or until most of the liquid has evaporated. Stir in the Madeira or Port and let reduce 3 to 5 minutes or until slightly syrupy. Stir in the cream and cook about 5 minutes or until thickened slightly. Remove from heat and stir in salt, pepper, and chives.

4. Combine mushrooms with the wild rice and spoon into warmed tortillas. Fold up burrito style and serve.

Makes 8 servings

Turkey Chili Burrito

2 tablespoons vegetable oil
2 medium onions, chopped
3 large garlic cloves, minced
2 jalapeño peppers, stemmed and chopped (including seeds) (see Note page 33)
1 tablespoon chili powder
1 teaspoon ground cumin
1 teaspoon ground coriander
1 pound ground turkey
1 16-ounce can white beans, drained and rinsed
1 17½-ounce can tomatoes in puree
2 tablespoons red wine vinegar
1 teaspoon salt
¼ teaspoon freshly ground black pepper
1 cup grated sharp cheddar cheese
½ cup chopped green onions
16 flour tortillas, warmed

1. Place oil in a medium saucepan over high heat. When hot, add the onions and cook, stirring constantly, 5 to 7 minutes or until they just start to brown slightly. Add the garlic, jalapeños, chili, cumin, and coriander. Cook, stirring occasionally with a wooden spoon, 3 to 5 minutes or until fragrant.

2. Add the turkey meat and cook, breaking up turkey with a fork, 5 to 10 minutes or until browned. Add the beans, tomatoes, vinegar, salt, and pepper. Bring to a boil, reduce heat to medium-low, cover, and simmer 40 minutes or until very thick.

3. Spoon the chili into warmed tortillas, sprinkle with grated cheddar and green onions, then roll up burrito style and serve.

Makes 8 servings

Southern Pecan Pie Burrito

1 tablespoon butter, melted
2 tablespoons all-purpose flour
2 tablespoons sugar
3 eggs, lightly beaten
2 cups dark corn syrup
1 teaspoon vanilla extract
3 tablespoons dark rum
1 cup pecan halves
8 flour tortillas, warmed

1. Preheat the oven to 425° F. Brush an 8-inch pie pan with the butter.

2. In a large mixing bowl, sift together the flour and sugar. Stir in the eggs, corn syrup, vanilla, and rum. Put the pecans in the bottom of the prepared pan and pour corn syrup mixture over top.

3. Bake for 10 minutes, then reduce heat to 325° F. and continue to bake an additional 20 minutes or until a knife inserted in the center of the pie comes out clean. Spoon into warmed tortillas, roll up burrito style, and serve.

Makes 6 to 8 servings